FULL CIRCLE

A LIFE IN REBELLION

with Ben Morea + 1000 voices collective

edited by Ariel Uessler

DETRITUS BOOKS

FIRST DETRITUS BOOKS EDITION, 2025

Published in the USA by Detritus Books

Images courtesy of Boo-Hooray

Cover image: *Full Circle*, painting by Ben Morea, 1965

DETRITUS BOOKS
Olympia, WA
detritusbooks.com

Distributed by AK Press

DETRITUS BOOKS ISBN: 978-1-948501-32-3

Printed in Canada

DAY ONE: *a broader sense of politics* | 5

DAY TWO: *armed love* | 17

DAY THREE: *break into the real* | 31

DAY FOUR: *the militant line* | 39

DAY FIVE: *a family in struggle* | 49

DAY SIX: *freedom* | 61

DAY SEVEN: *(counter)revolution* | 73

DAY EIGHT: *wild west* | 79

DAY NINE: *Pancho Villa syndrome* | 89

DAY TEN: *revolutionary animism* | 101

DAY ELEVEN: *the will to live* | 109

DAY TWELVE: *go to the mountain* | 123

DAY THIRTEEN: *reconnecting* | 133

DAY FOURTEEN: *the great mystery* | 143

DAY FIFTEEN: *a life in rebellion* | 153

DAY SIXTEEN: *warrior* | 161

DAY SEVENTEEN: *karmically correct* | 171

DAY EIGHTEEN: *a way of life* | 187

DAY NINETEEN: *life as struggle* | 201

DAY TWENTY: *totality* | 213

DAY ONE

Ben, if you don't mind, we'd like to start from an early age, in your life before the Lower East Side.

It's not political.

No, it's political. It's already political.

Right, everything is political. Life is political. I just said that meaning, it's more biographical. It might not be of any interest.

But I could start from an early age. I grew up in a city project, from a poor family. It was mostly Black and Puerto Rican, in an area called San Juan Hill. That was the north end of Hell's Kitchen. A lot of musicians lived there. Thelonious Monk lived there, I used to go to his house. Miles Davis lived there. There were a lot of Cuban musicians. It was really a music area. So growing up, I was involved with music. I started off as a teenager playing jazz. But I got addicted to heroin.

Heroin was really common?

It was big in the '40s and '50s. It was major. And jazz was all heroin. So I kept getting arrested, and I'd be in jail and I'd — they used the term "cold turkey," meaning to break your addiction without medical help, without drugs to bring you down. And one time when I was in jail, my liver gave out. I was dying, my liver was completely infected. So they moved me to a prison hospital.

But you were really young, right?

I was. But I'd been using heroin since I was 15 years old. Then, while I was in the prison hospital, I had a therapist that took an interest in me, and she tried to help me. She said to me, "this is the third time you've done this, cold turkey, been in jail and kicked the habit, then you go out and you start again." She said, "you're gonna do it again unless — why don't you leave the jazz world? Why don't you find another expression, try painting as your form of art?" Because she understood that if I stayed in the jazz world, I would go back to heroin. So, as therapy, she started me painting. And I'm still painting, sixty years later.

I never went back to heroin after that. I kept painting, and I got involved with the artists in the Lower East Side. I had a mentor, I met an older artist that took interest in my work. He just died last week. Aldo Tambellini. He was ten or eleven years older than me. I'm like a descendant of his.

Anyway so we formed a group of artists, called Group Center. We were opposed to the commodification of art, and tried to find ways to present art that wasn't about commerce.

Were you critical of the abstract expressionists, like Pollock or Rothko?

No. I was critical of what was replacing abstract art: pop art. I hated it. The abstract expressionists believed in art, as a necessity in life. Commercial interests gained control by making it a product. But the artists themselves still believed in expression. The pop artists, though, were completely commercial. They believed in money and fame.

With Group Center we took the approach of showing art in non-commercial spaces, also combining music, poetry, dance, all the different media. I did the music, I created instruments out of machines. I'd always been interested in music, and I started using machines to make music. And so I worked with them for a couple years. But meanwhile I became more and more political. And there was another artist in the group that moved in the same direction. So he and I decided to start Black Mask, which was an effort to combine art and politics.

When you say that you became more political, what did that mean to you?

It just became more of a focus. Back in the jazz days, I also had a social consciousness. Because I was in the projects, mostly with Black people, I was aware of the lie of the American dream. I could see that something was wrong. I was part of the underclass. Though I had limited political consciousness of that, it was a visceral anger toward the suppression of people.

As I became more politically conscious, I became more conscious of the problems in the world. I always felt close to the struggles in Black America, that was very important. At some point I got involved in the anti-Vietnam War struggle, and that became really important. When we started Black Mask, we felt that at that moment in America, we were also fighting against the war in Vietnam, and we were fighting alongside the Black population. Black Mask was an expression of that.

What year was that, when Black Mask started?

It was 1965 or '66. It's hard to say exactly. The journal started in '66. But there were only ten issues. It existed only two years.

It was just the two of you?

In the beginning it was mainly just two of us that put the journal together. But as we did things around the city it would attract people, and sometimes those people would join us. Like when we shut down MOMA — that was our first action. We weren't a big group, but we did involve a lot of people.

Eventually we'd like to ask about the different relations you were able to make, from the Black Panthers to the Weather Underground, to Valerie Solanas, also you knew the Living Theater, the Diggers, Situationists...It's like a compendium of '60s radicals! For example I was surprised to learn, you knew Yuri Kochiyama? For me it's so important to learn about these connections.

That's the most ironic thing: Yuri also lived in the project. I met her when I was really young. I can't remember how we met exactly. I just remember that she was nice to me, like she would always say hi and try to talk to me, you know. She was really sweet to me. I was a kid, maybe 13, 14. She was older, like a mother.

Actually you didn't meet through politics, but because you lived in the same place.

Correct. But what's so ironic is that we met again, years later. When I was more political, after I'd left the project. And she was living in Harlem, and she was involved with Malcolm X. She was very close to Malcolm.

I know she was there when he was killed.

She held him as he died. But so when we met again, when we re-met, we hadn't seen each other in years. I had become completely political, and she was surprised like "ohhh it's you!" And she invited me to her home uptown, in Harlem. I used to go up there for meetings with Black radicals and militants. Everyone there was Black except for me and her.

But when you were younger, she didn't tell you anything political, she was just like a friendly neighbor woman?

Right. To be honest with you, I never was clear how it came about. I can't recall how we met the second time. Like I don't remember our conversation, or how she recognized that I was that same kid. And I always wondered how she realized that I had reached a similar political understanding, that was parallel to hers. I don't know if she saw me with *Black Mask* maybe, cuz I used to be on the street with it in the Village...I can't remember where I came across her. It's really a blur.

That's really mysterious. So then after Black Mask, you started Up Against the Wall Motherfucker?

Correct. But we didn't name it that. To call yourself "Up Against the Wall Motherfucker" is almost pretentious. We didn't have a name. But the first thing we did was to bring garbage to Lincoln Center.

There was a garbage strike throughout the city. So in the poor areas like the Lower East Side, the garbage was over the ceiling. In the rich areas there were private carting services. And so we decided that was unfair, they should have some garbage too. I mean maybe they're missing it. So we decided to bring garbage from the Lower East Side up to Lincoln Center and dump it in the wading pool. We made a leaflet announcing that we were going to do it. We called it a cultural exchange: *garbage for garbage*.

But then, how should we sign the leaflet? We didn't have a name. It was just this group that had formed around Black Mask. It had no identity yet. It had no ideology; it was just radical. I was friends with LeRoi Jones, aka Amiri Baraka, and he had written a poem that said "up against the wall motherfucker." We said "why don't we put that, like a revolutionary slogan?" So we wrote that on the leaflet. We didn't intend it as a name, but everybody who saw it thought that it was our name. And it kind of stuck.

"Up against the wall" means like hitting against something?

It's not a metaphor. It's literal. It meant you had to stand against the wall with your hands up. Like when the police arrested somebody, especially in the ghetto, they'd say "up against the wall, motherfucker!" Or if somebody was gonna rob you they'd say "up against the wall!" So it was a common expression in the ghetto. Both police and criminals, everybody used it.

You know, I hesitate to use the word "criminal." It's not that some people are just criminals. Poverty makes crime. People in poverty turn to crime. So naturally in the ghetto, there are people who are criminalized.

In your case, and for other radicals also, there's an existential sympathy with criminals. Would you think of them as revolutionary?

Sometimes. They're rebellious. They're definitely oppositional. They may not theoretically be revolutionaries. But in their very existence, they're against the imposed order.

A lot of criminals become revolutionary, at certain times. Even classic examples that everybody knows, like Robin Hood. They lived in the forest that the ruling class of England thought they owned. Part of that was their resistance. There's always this interplay between revolutionary and criminal, and living against the law.

Then the target of rebellion is the wealth itself, held by the ruling class.

And it's interesting — actually Lincoln Center was built where I grew up. That was San Juan Hill. The project is still there, but all the ghetto housing was torn down. They destroyed it to build Lincoln Center. So that was also part of the reason for doing what we did. It wasn't stated, but that was definitely part of it.

Lincoln Center used to be San Juan Hill? Around the west 60s?

Right, it was the north end of Hell's Kitchen. See the southern end of Hell's Kitchen was all Italian, from 37th to 42nd. My mother was born there. Then when it got to 42nd it turned Irish. From 42nd to 57th was totally Irish. Then from 57th up it became mixed. And that was San Juan Hill. There was a large Black population, there were Italians, Irish, Greek, some Puerto Ricans had started moving in. It was a viable mixed community, where a lot of musicians and cultural people lived. Thelonious Monk! Miles Davis! It was a cultural haven. And they destroyed it to put up an edifice to culture, which was its exact opposite.

So there was a double reason for doing what we did. It showed what we thought of Western culture.

I had no idea. I'd never even heard the name San Juan Hill before. It's like they erased it from historical memory.

There's almost no one left that knows what it was like.

The Lower East Side must have been so different back then, too.

It was a ghetto. Mainly Black and Puerto Rican, and Ukrainian. And a lot of artists lived there, poets, theater people. It was a center of the counterculture, it drew a lot of people. So it was diverse.

That was the setting for your political activity, like neighborhood-based community organizing?

But we had a different orientation. We never thought of ourselves as organizers. You know, the Marxists were always talking about organizing, but we were the exact opposite. We weren't trying to organize anything! We were trying to live free. And that would attract people, and it would show an example of what this could be — to live free. So in a sense it was organizational. But it wasn't organization.

I've always been curious about the word "free." It seems like in the '60s it had a real meaning. But today hardly anyone uses it, except for the right wing. For you "live free" meant like something outside of capitalism and bureaucracy?

Your life was controlled by you. Not by an outside force. So that meant economic freedom, cultural freedom, spiritual freedom, artistic freedom. We wanted people to be free, totally. Not just in the anti-capitalist sense. We hardly ever even used the word "capitalism." It was obvious that to be free you would be opposed to capitalism. But that's not the main objective. The main objective is to build the alternative. It's so subtle, the difference.

It was more a positive orientation, rather than just oppositional. We were always oriented towards what we could do to make our life more free, rather than what we could do to oppose those who want to make us less free. Like when we cut the fence at Woodstock — a lot of people don't realize, Woodstock was not intended to be a free event. There were fences where you had to pay. So we cut the fence! And a politico might say, "so what? Big deal, you cut the fence." But it was a way of showing, this is our culture. It's not a commodity. It wasn't made to make somebody wealthy. It was made for us to share.

It was more about empowering people to act, than to contest the powers that be?

But it's both. To emphasize that, I always compare two things we did. The first was cutting the fence at Woodstock. The second, another thing that we did, was breaking into the Pentagon.

That was during the March on the Pentagon, right? You actually managed to break in!

We were the first people in history to do it! Probably the last. So obviously, that is a very militant act. Most political people would say "oh that's the right thing, attack the Pentagon." But to me, they were equal. It's not that one was better than the other. They were both important.

Because it wasn't just political, economic control that we opposed, but all control, cultural, spiritual...Like, religion is control. It's taking spirituality and using it to repress people. Spirituality should be freeing people. Everybody should be spiritual. But religion uses it, and it becomes another form of control.

So from the standpoint of freedom, both actions are equal.

Totally. It was an effort to live free. To express our freedom as people. And everything we did was like that. Like feeding people, I mean we fed people all the time. We'd have big feasts in the Lower East Side with hundreds of people, several times a week! It wasn't organizing like "we have to organize people." But rather, communize people.

Were there ever schisms in the group, with some people saying "no we have to be more organized," or different ideas about would be more revolutionary?

That's not how we were. We didn't have to all agree. To be honest with you, I can't even say that everybody in Up Against the Wall was an anarchist. We didn't have an ideology.

How many of you were there?

In the core there might have been forty or fifty. But around them were another hundred. And then around them were another hundred. It's like the ripples when you throw a stone in water. So that was not...We weren't interested in numbers.

You weren't interested in growing as organization, or influence?

Right. We didn't do things to build our importance. We were not trying to be important. We were trying to live.

That sounds like a real power. You weren't fixated on a certain effect; your activity was more open-ended.

That's why the politicos didn't like us. We always had this mixed style. Art was always there in the politics, and poetry, and spirituality. It was never just organizational politics. It was the broadest sense of politics, which is life.

That's another answer to the question of what it means to be political. It's a different conception of politics.

Also, what's been lost is the sense of relativity. Like with political correctness. It's an absolute, it's not relative. But absoluteness has no place in life.

For instance, I was allied with the Black Panthers. But they had an authoritarian streak, and I was opposed to that authoritarianism. Yet I was fighting beside them in the struggle against the larger oppressor, America. I made it clear to them: I'm opposed to authoritarianism. Someday, when we're successful, we can fight it out. But for now, if it's America or you, I'm with you!

See that's why you need relativity. But there were some people who felt like I shouldn't be pro-Black Panther, just on principle.

It's a problem of ideological purism?

And if you're absolute, it sometimes prevents you from coming to the right conclusions. Because you reject something based on whether it fits your ideology. Like sometimes I worked with Black nationalists. I'm not in support of nationalism. But we all wanted the same goal — to reshape American racial reality.

In other words, rather than making decisions based only on ideology, you have to think through each instance. It's not about being politically correct. You must be able to understand what you are choosing between, and base your choice on those possibilities. Case by case, you have to be capable of deciding… But it's hard for the modern young mind to understand that. Relativity today is almost gone. And it's so important to bring back that sense. Because when you lose the sense of relativity, then you're unable to act. It's a very subtle thing.

Today we heard two important concepts, relátivity and freedom. I've always wondered about that word. We don't hear it anymore. Maybe the meaning that it had in the '60s was lost.

Because people become so obsessed with the idea of opposition, they forget what it is they're opposing. What's the goal.

What makes it hard to keep the sense of relativity, do you think?

A lot of it has to do with control. If your thinking is absolute, you're easier to control. And the authoritarian Left can control people by stressing opposition alone. But relativity allows for less control. It gives you, as a person, freedom of choice. You're not bound by dogma and ideology, but by what you feel better leads to freedom.

And you really can't control what you feel. It's beyond that.

Right. And relativity gives you the freedom to feel the depth of something. Not just what you call it, but what it really is.

TO LIVE ONE MUST LOVE
TO LOVE ONE MUST SURVIVE
TO SURVIVE ONE MUST FIGHT!

-MOTHERFUCKERS- I.W.W.C.

DAY TWO

Today we're hoping you might tell us some stories from everyday life in the Lower East Side. Like what you were eating, where you were living...how did you all get by?

Well, there's a lot of gray area there. You know, we were thieves. Especially the women, they were really good at it. So a lot of our food was stolen. At the same time, we fed people. We had non-profit papers that I got from one of the liberal churches, so we could go to the markets and get day-old food for free. Then we had people who cooked, and we'd get church halls, or meeting halls in the neighborhood. We could have three or four hundred people come for dinner! We did that maybe two or three nights a week.

We also raised money. We had what we called crash pads where we could put people up, so that there were free places for people to stay. Like we would find runaways on the street and we'd give them the address. We had multiple crash pads where people could stay. And we also stayed in some of them. So we didn't have much rent.

Were the crash pads squatted?

Some. Mostly we paid rent. But the Lower East Side rent was cheap, we're talking less than fifty dollars a month. And we raised money, we had a fund to feed and house people, and different people would contribute. At one point, all the dope dealers in the Lower East Side — not hard drugs like heroin, but the grass and psychedelic dealers contributed to it.

Interesting, why would they do that?

We were building a community. And that concerned them too. See the Lower East Side was like a Mecca, it was drawing people. So the dealers were making money. And some of them would contribute to a fund for the community, because they also benefitted from the community. So we used to encourage that. We were always raising money.

It sounds like a big operation.

It was. We had the free food, and the crash pads, generally we had several crash pads. We had a free store, where people could get clothes for free. There was a bail fund so we could bail people out of jail. We had lawyers, and doctors, on retainer. It was extensive!

How did you manage the money? I assume it was cash.

I don't know, different people handled it. I never did. But it was a lot of cash. The dope dealers, everybody mainly used cash.

Raising money was important, but that was only part of it. It wasn't all based on that. I'll give you an example, to show how we operated. You know how yogurt is sold in a container, and it's labeled, say like strawberry. Well, when it goes through the machines, sometimes the machine misses the strawberry, so they can't sell it and they throw it away. We found out that Dannon was throwing away thousands of these containers every week — of good yogurt! And we had a refrigerator at a crash pad that we weren't really using, so we started going every week, we had a fifty-five gallon drum and we would fill it with yogurt! We would take it out to the street on a cart and wheel it around, and people could get free yogurt.

You'd open each container?

Open each container and put the yogurt in the barrel.

But why open them, why not leave it in the container?

That way people could take a few spoons, or as much as they wanted. And it was an energy. It looked cool, I mean, a barrel full of yogurt! Plus it was easier to handle.

Then at some point, I don't know if Dannon decided to give us more, or they were making more mistakes, but at some point they had twice as much yogurt as we'd been getting. So I thought "well we need another refrigerator. But how are we going to get a refrigerator?" I said "I don't know, but let's go. We'll just go walk around."

As we were walking around, we saw a place that sold appliances. Outside they had some refrigerators. But you know how heavy refrigerators are. So I went inside and I asked them "do you have a cart?" Of course they did. So I asked if I could rent it. They said "yes if you leave a deposit." I said "okay," and I took the cart. As I was leaving, I passed the refrigerators outside. There were three or four guys ready. They put the refrigerator on the cart and we went off!

We didn't think of it as stealing. Like the Robin Hood consciousness, we thought of it as liberating from those who have it and passing it to those who need it. It was not theft for our own aggrandizement.

Did you have a name for this kind of activity, or you just did it?

Well people knew Up Against the Wall. Then we had a name, like for the nonprofit papers we used the name East Side Survival Organization, ESSO. Like the oil company.

That's funny. So it was ironic.

Yeah, and we used to have a sign that mimicked the Esso logo. We had it up on the free store.

But you know, we weren't trying to be a charity. For example in the free store, we had free clothing. So people would come in and get clothes for free. At the same time, we had a printing press. And AWOL soldiers would come in and get clothes, and false ID. It wasn't a matter of getting something for free. It was about the possibility that life could be free!

Where was the free store, by the way?

East 10th Street. We had one around Avenue B, by Tompkins Square Park. Then we moved to a bigger one around 3rd Avenue. And we started squatting. See we rented the free store, which was the street level, and the rest of the building on top of it was empty. So we broke the lock and took over the building! Since we'd already been there in the free store, people were used to seeing us around.

It must have been a lively spot, people coming and going.

Oh yeah, people hung out there all day. There was a group that used to call themselves the Wine Group for Freedom. They were semi-homeless, like street people, mostly Black and Puerto Rican, and they would hang around. And we were always doing things around the neighborhood, like at St. Marks we would have free food, we'd have concerts in Tompkins Square Park, maybe every other week we would get bands to donate their time and play free concerts. We were always doing things.

How about Canned Heat, you were friends with them right? Did they play in the park?

Yeah, Canned Heat were my friends. They didn't play at the park, but they played at the Fillmore, when we got the Fillmore one night a week. That's another thing we did. We occupied the Fillmore East and forced Bill Graham to give us use of the theater, one night a week, to put on free concerts for people. A lot of rock bands came and played, including Sly and the Family Stone, the MC5 and Country Joe McDonald.

But when we did things in the neighborhood, like the concerts in Tompkins Square Park, we always took the effort to make it multicultural. We would never only have rock concerts. We thought that would be insulting, what about these other people that were there? So we had rock bands, but we would also have Latin bands, as well as Black bands and steel drums. So that there would be a neighborhood-wide representation. We were really conscious about that, not to cater only to the white population of hippies. We saw it all as one community.

It was a heterogeneous composition of people.

Totally. Some were white, some Native American, some Black, some Puerto Rican. And there were different groups in the community, there were street people, there were hippies and new age people. There were artists, poets, theater people, there were students. And within our group, there were different groupings. We were consciously very mixed.

Like the students for example. Since we helped with the occupation of Columbia University, a lot of students oriented towards us. And they had their own identity, their own way of being. So they would stay together, most of them would stay in the same crash pad. We all hung out together, ate together, did things together. But certain crash pads were more student, or more dropout, or more street people. We didn't tell anyone where to stay. People would find their own grouping.

What was the age range, it was mainly younger people?

It was all ages. Young people, old people, teenagers, even kids! There were runaways that stayed with us, some as young as 10 or 12 years old. We'd find them on the street and put them up, if they wouldn't go back home. We would encourage them to go home but they would not, so we took care of them. We had a lot of them. There were crash pads where the kids could stay, as well as some of us that were older.

So there were multiple generations. In fact, we thought of our group as family. It wasn't an organization. We didn't call it "Up Against the Wall." We just called it the family.

How about you, where did you stay?

I'd never stay in the same crash pad more than a couple nights. I was constantly moving. So that my whereabouts remained unknown.

At that point you were already underground?

I was off the grid, so to speak.

What were your interactions with the cops like?

It depended on the situation. They were always hassling people, trying to bust people, you know, as cops always do. But we were extremely volatile. So how we responded, often depended on how hard we were pushed.

Say there was a bust and they arrested a bunch of people. Then we would call for a demo, and that night a hundred people might show up at the precinct. Sometimes it would turn into a riot, and they'd arrest more people. Then the next day we'd be back at it again.

We had our own mimeograph machine that we used to make leaflets and fliers. So when something happened that we wanted people to know about, we could write a leaflet and immediately print it. I'll show you...Like these, we'd print hundreds of these and pass them out around the neighborhood.

I love these. "News from the streets!"

That's really what it was. Sometimes we'd take the mimeograph out with us, we'd make a leaflet and print it right there on the street!

It's great to see these. It's like looking back into another time: "heads," "freaks," "the hip community." Did you identify with the hippies?

The term "hippie" was more of a media invention. We preferred the term "freak." Actually, some of us were from an earlier generation, some of us came from the Beats. We were in the new age, what people call hippie counterculture. But we were older, with more Beat influence.

By appearance, we dressed a bit like hippies, and we had long hair. So we looked more or less like hippies, and we were around them. All these dropouts were moving to the Lower East Side, and they were a part of the community we were building. But you could feel that there was a difference. We had an edge. You know, the city was rough. And a lot of us had been criminalized as youth. We didn't fit with the love generation, we weren't flower children. Instead of peace and love, we proposed "armed love" — I coined that phrase.

You were armed yourselves, right? You carried guns?

Correct. In other words, we were not pacifists. We believed in self-defense, and that could mean violence. So the real, hardcore hippies didn't trust us, or they were apprehensive of us, because of that. But to most political people, we were outsiders. Like some Marxists hated us! You know, we used LSD and hung out in the streets. So we were in this weird middle ground. And that was the beauty of our family. There was almost nobody like us.

What was their problem with LSD and hanging out in the street?

They were opposed to the culture. They looked down on it, they wanted nothing to do with it. They saw it as apolitical. And they dismissed the whole psychedelic, new age movement. Whereas we felt that the counterculture, combined with a political understanding, was where we were going.

At that time there was a division, either you were political or you were psychedelic. And what made us different was that we were both. I mean there was no other group like us. We were militants, committed to revolutionary struggle. And we were totally part of the alternative, psychedelic world.

Because you recognized that as an important force.

But it wasn't just a decision, like "we better go join this world." We were part of it, we believed in it. As psychedelic people, we believed that the mind had to be changed, as well as the body.

Will you say more? How did the psychedelic movement play into the struggle?

It was part of the larger struggle to find a way to live outside of the norm. And it was really important. People left the suburbs and white middle-class America, because they were psychedelicized! America was at the point of change, and psychedelics were part of it. And we were part of that energy.

Did you ever use LSD in actions?

It had nothing to do with street action. It was just part of our life.

Did you take psychedelics together, though?

Not necessarily together, it was up to a person. It wasn't planned. Sometimes I would take them and just walk around the streets. Or a couple of us would go down on the weekend to Wall Street, when there's no people, no cars, and we'd walk around. We'd get on the ferry and go out, you know, it was organic.

But did you feel that using psychedelics could help, like maybe they were good for relationships between people?

I didn't believe in the concept of doing something for a result. We just lived it. And we believed in change.

See, the mind is programmed. There's no way to avoid it. And we realized that if you want to rewire your mind, you're going to need something. That's what LSD was useful for. To rewire, and shatter illusion.

Yet for some people, LSD couldn't help. In some cases it even hurt. Some people were so damaged mentally that when they saw the way out, it was more frightening than being in. Really it's tragic. That's why we were vehemently opposed to the idea of dosing people, meaning to give someone acid without their knowledge. They did it a lot on the West Coast, like Ken Kesey and them with the acid tests. Kool-aid acid, that's what it was: a bowl of Kool-aid full of acid that they just set out somewhere, and people may drink it without knowing. Could you imagine, you think you're in the regular world, then all of a sudden it shatters? It could shatter you! I mean it's deadly. It's like killing someone, to dose them. So we were adamantly opposed to it. Something that drastic, you have to choose it, consciously. You have to be ready for it. You have to be aware of what could happen.

But in general, we encouraged the use of acid. We didn't see it as a cure all, as Tim Leary did. But we saw that it was helping to question one's place in society and in the universe. Although I eventually came to feel that psychotropics are a better avenue.

Psychotropics?

In other words not the man-made chemical, but plants like psilocybin, ayahuasca, you know there's all kinds that are part of nature.

I see. How did you encourage acid use, specifically?

We used the distinction between "life drugs" and "death drugs." Death drugs were hard drugs like heroin and speed. Many of us had had problems with death drugs and saw that they were destructive. Whereas we saw that life drugs were promoting life — namely psychedelics, also grass and hashish, and psychotropics.

So when we had the free night at the Fillmore, that gave us a chance to distinguish. That was another thing that was disturbing to some Leftists, we actually distributed life drugs throughout the theater, for free! Because we wanted to make it clear. Life drugs, we advocated. We promoted them. Death drugs we were totally opposed to. We wouldn't let them in the door! We would not allow anybody to come in and distribute death drugs.

The way you talk about the Lower East Side, it sounds like you played a protective role toward a lot of people.

We did. We felt protective of the youth coming from the suburbs. We didn't want them to become victims. You know, the Lower East Side was rough. I mean it was a ghetto. And all these runaways and young kids were out on the streets. And they could be preyed on.

There were a lot of runaways?

Hundreds of them! Some were really young kids, that had just run away from home. They had no idea what this world they just entered was. We had armed patrols every night, walking around to make sure the kids were alright. We were out there and if we saw some we asked them, "do you have a place to stay?" And we'd give them an address where we had a crash pad, and tell them "you could stay there, you'll be safe."

Which means, the government didn't help these kids?

No. And the thought was, we want to do it for ourselves. We want to set up a separate, independent community. We protect our own people — even from police. We don't need police.

It's a bad expression, but it's like the Lower East Side was really your territory back then.

It was. It went from 1st Street up to 14th Street, that was the northern edge. And from 3rd Avenue all the way to Avenue D.

That's pretty much the whole Lower East Side! You must have had a powerful presence.

We did. Like one night, we barricaded the streets and threw a party. We had hundreds of people out in the streets. The cops showed up, but there were so many of us that they gave up! They turned around and left.

Eventually we got too strong, and the cops starting busting us for everything they could. But for a time, the cops couldn't control us.

So the heyday was the 1960s, up until '68 or '69 I guess?

'60s, correct.

But then, at some point you left the city, or it became untenable to stay. Was it hard to give up that territory? Or how did you think about it?

Well, it's complex. It was a situation where I had to leave. But there was also something somebody once said to me, that always stood in the back of my mind: this is their world. We can fight them, and we can resist, and we can rebel. But they think it's their world.

At some point we reached the conclusion that, if we wanted to have an alternative world, we would have to build it.

A lot of you left together? What year was that?

I personally left the city in '69 (under a legal cloud). Some people stayed a little longer. Some left when I left.

Then what happened?

It took forty years until I came back. And in those forty years, I learned a lot. I went somewhere else. I tried to find what another life might look like. And now after forty years, I'm trying to bring what I learned back.

Eventually we'd like to ask more about those forty years. Of course, some things you may not want to talk about.

If it gets to that point I'll just say I can't talk about it. Or I'll talk about it in a guarded way.

It does seem like many of your concepts, I know they were there from the '60s, but maybe you're seeing them through this other lens as well?

Right. It's not that I abandoned one and I embraced another. It's that they became one. For example my psychedelic life before, and my psychotropic life now, have become one.

But I'm running out of time.

I'm so glad that we have this time with you now. Thank you, Ben. It's getting exciting!

I'm excited about it also.

BLACK MASK

No. 2 DEC. 1966 5 Cents

The Total Revolution

One continuing purpose of this newsletter will be to fuse fractionalized struggles into a functional whole. Too long we have witnessed the weakening and eventual destruction of radical movements by their forced specialization. Obviously one must function within an area of personal confrontation be it the factory, the ghetto, or the university, but there must always be the inner direction of a totality. The labor unions concern only with wages and working conditions has all but emasculated their original radicalism. The negro movement for integration would have fallen into the same trap, but now the cry of "Black Power" will put an emphasis on community control, revitalizing their struggle, just as the goal of workers control of production, especially under the impending changes of automation and cybernation,

DAY THREE

You know, Ben, nowadays it's commonplace for activists to think of art and performance, in conjunction with action. But in your time, it was just starting. You were one of those who initiated performative, situational art.

But not I alone. Before Black Mask, there was Group Center. And the person who organized that was Aldo Tambellini. Aldo had developed a multimedia presentation, that combined visual art, music, jazz, poetry, dance... And that was performed in public, non-commercial spaces, like at St. Mark's Church in the Bowery, and at the Film Anthology. We did that maybe ten times, in '64 and '65.

What we did involved a slide projector, Aldo would paint on the slides. So when you put the slide in the machine it would heat up and the paint would start to move, you'd see it move in the projection. Then as Aldo showed the slides and the paint was moving, I had these sound machines, I created instruments out of machines that I used to make music. Plus we had a live musician, a jazz bassist, so he and I would improvise. Also there was a dancer, a woman with Twyla Tharp's group, Judith Dunn. And a poet, Calvin Hernton, he was a Black poet. He was really strong.

That was relatively early for that genre of performance art, like mixed media, multimedia...Is that what you called it at the time?

Multimedia, correct. We were one of the first as far as I know. So a lot of artists were influenced by it, like "wow, multimedia!" For us the point was to present art as a part of life — not a commodity.

It's important also that you did it in the Lower East Side, to share it with people there.

We felt that was important. We believed art is a necessity. I still do. I always say that art is like breathing. It's not an object. It's a way of being.

But as I was working with Group Center, I began to feel that something was missing. Art alone was not enough. I was very concerned with the political struggles happening at that time, especially in Black America, and against the war in Vietnam. More and more I felt the need to join art and politics in a revolutionary struggle. There was another artist in the group, Ron Hahne, who shared that feeling. And that was when we started Black Mask. We didn't break with Aldo. But we went in a different direction. And that was a move out of the art world.

Black Mask was a way of making art that was more explicitly political?

But we didn't just want to make political art. The point was that it wasn't enough to be an artist and just make art. In a sense, we wanted to eliminate the separation between art and politics, and life. We felt that what was necessary was a total revolution.

Our emphasis from the beginning was the idea of totality. It was a way of saying that this whole thing has to change. It's not sufficient to just change it politically, or aesthetically. To make a real change, to change reality, we have to change the way of life itself.

Western society has reached a stalemate and needs a complete overhaul. We knew that wasn't going to happen, but that was our goal. That was what we were about.

Black Mask targeted institutional centers of art and culture. Would you talk about some of those actions?

Our first action as a group was to close down MOMA. We announced that we were going to do that, and why. Then they actually closed the museum preemptively, fearing our action! When we got there, they had already locked the doors. We just put up a sign saying *MUSEUM CLOSED.*

At other times we would disrupt exhibitions and galleries, to raise issues we felt were pertinent. Once after disrupting a lecture at NYU, I was challenged to a debate by some of the academics. It was a pretentious event that was only meant for the cultural elite. So we made a leaflet advertising a party with free food and alcohol, we went down to the Bowery and handed out leaflets to all the drunks and street people. They had to block off the streets because so many people showed up!

That's hilarious.

It was a true Dadaist sense of humor. A lot of the actions we did were thought up on the spot. We weren't like most political groups with grandiose strategies and plans. For us the actions were a way of expressing ourselves, and seeing how we could make a dent in society.

That's a nice way to think about action, as a mode of expression. And a way of moving while questioning.

And that was a way for us to understand our place in the ongoing struggle. But eventually, I reached a point where Black Mask and the idea of bringing art and politics together was no longer enough.

I pushed to street activism — or street action took over. That was when Black Mask evolved into Up Against the Wall.

In other words, you entered a new realm of struggle. How did you distinguish it from the earlier period with Black Mask?

I knew it wasn't enough to write about it anymore. It was time to go into the streets.

Did you stop painting too?

Yes, there was no time or room for it. We were in the middle of a struggle! It wasn't part-time. It was daily. It was a life. We even put out an announcement that said "we're gonna stop publishing *Black Mask*: it's time to go into the streets!"

Black Mask did have a presence in the streets, though, it wasn't just the publication.

But the publication shaped the effort. In reality Black Mask and Up Against the Wall were very different, in terms of the people involved, and what they did. Black Mask was much smaller. It was more of an esoteric group. And I was the central force. Whereas in Up Against the Wall, there was no center. It included people from all persuasions that wanted to live a life more real, and more visceral. In a sense, it was more vital. It was also extremely volatile.

It wasn't that we reorganized from one group to another. We experienced an organic movement of effort. It just changed. It grew. At some point, Up Against the Wall became a living organism. And at some point Black Mask just became less relevant. So when we put out the statement that we were stopping Black Mask to go into the streets, that wasn't an organizational effort. It was a real transformation — we lived it. It was time, and there was an opening. The struggle moved from pen and paper, into the street itself.

But still, Black Mask was important. It was historic!

It was major.

Because it's not just the written analysis but also the style, like the Wall Street action and that image of masked protesters dressed all in black, that influenced the later generation of black bloc, no? The French and American black bloc, and the German Autonomen, seem to have followed this style of militancy.

And not just style, there were certain tactics. Like one that we used, we called the breakaway. We would go to demonstrations looking for an opening, and then break. That's what black bloc picked up on.

"Breakaway" precisely means to break away from the main group?

Correct. When we started doing breakaways in the '60s, at that time there were a lot of mass demonstrations and protests. To us, the concept of protest was ridiculous. As if it was sufficient to go to a march and carry a sign. We were not into protesting; we were into changing. As militants, we were ready for direct confrontation. And that was the point of the breakaway.

That was part of the action at the Pentagon, right? Was that a breakaway?

Exactly. We went and looked for an opening. That's when we broke into the Pentagon. Literally! In other words, that was the ultimate breakaway.

It's also very scary. I mean who can break into the Pentagon? It's no joke.

Who would even think like that now, that you could even try it? And we didn't know, when we went there, that we were going to do it. We didn't know what we were going to do. But we knew we were going to do something.

It was during a big demonstration against the Vietnam War, that was supposed to be one of the biggest at that time. So there was a lot of build up to it. And the counterculture figures were gonna go and levitate the Pentagon. We said "come on, you know, that's ridiculous." Then we said "we've got to go. That's it, we're going!"

Before we got there, we had tried to get all the people that we thought were more militant together. That way if something opened, we would be together. And at some point — we had reconnoitered and found that there was a side door — and at some point we saw that this door was left unguarded. There were no troops, the troops were all in the front. It was totally unguarded. So we moved our part of the crowd to the side toward this door, we started running and we charged it. And we broke in! We fought our way in.

A lot of people were part of it?

Hundreds! There's a film by Chris Marker that shows it. You can see all of a sudden there's hundreds of people charging — that's when we breach it. Then it shows us being beaten out. When the troops realized that we had gotten in, they charged us from inside. That's where a lot of blood was spilled.

But how it happened, actually, we worked on it for months. I had a Japanese friend, a guy from the Zengakuren that came and stayed with me for a while. He went by the name Charlie. He and I went around to different groups, like we went to SDS, we went to the Trotskyists, we went to all these different groups to present the idea of the breakaway. And we tried to get them to congregate, if they were interested in taking part, we specified the area where we were gonna meet. So that if the moment came that a breakaway was possible, we would be in a larger number.

So actually, a lot of preparation went into it.

We worked on it for months! Just Charlie and I. Otherwise up until then we'd been doing breakaways during every demonstration, but it was just twenty or thirty of us. We wanted to make a bigger impact at the Pentagon.

Then after that, where do you go from there? I mean that was the ultimate breakaway, so you kind of reached a limit, probably you couldn't do a bigger one. But did you try for a second one? I wonder how you thought about it tactically.

We didn't work like that. We didn't organize or plan, like "we're gonna repeat this." We would just see what the next event was and be ready. Like when we saw there was going to be this thing at the Pentagon, then it became clear that we could do something. We didn't know what, exactly. We just knew that we would do something. In other words, we were more spontaneous.

More situational.

Almost, in a sense, more artistic.

WE PROPOSE A CULTURE EXCHANGE:

(garbage for garbage)

AMERICA TURNS THE WORLD INTO GARBAGE
IT TURNS ITS GHETTOS INTO GARBAGE
IT TURNS VIETNAM INTO GARBAGE

IN THE NAME OF UNIVERSAL PRINCIPLES (DEMOCRACY, HUMAN RIGHTS)
IN THE NAME OF THE FATHERLAND (COLLIE DOGS, NEW ENGLAND CHURCHS)
IN THE NAME OF MAN IN THE NAME OF ART
IN THE NAME OF MONEY

AMERICA TAKES
ALL THAT IS EDIBLE, EXCHANGEABLE, INVESTABLE,
AND LEAVES THE REST

THE WORLD IS OUR GARBAGE. WE SHALL NOT WANT. WE LIE DOWN IN GREEN PASTURES. THE REST LIE DOWN IN GARBAGE

AND WE PLAY AS WE MAKE OUR GARBAGE
BEETHOVEN BACH MOZART SHAKESPEARE
TO COVER THE SOUND OF OUR GARBAGE MAKING

AND WE EXCLUDE THE GARBAGE FROM OUR PALACES OF CULTURE
AND WE WILL NOT ALLOW IT TO MARRY OUR DAUGHTER
AND WE WILL NOT NEGOTIATE WITH IT OR LET IT TAKE OUR SHIPS

BUT WE ARE FACED WITH A REVOLT OF THE GARBAGE

A CULTURAL REVOLUTION
GARBAGE FERTILIZES
DISCOVERS ITSELF

AND WE OF THE LOWER EAST SIDE HAVE DECIDED TO BRING
THIS CULTURAL REVOLUTION TO LINCOLN CENTER - IN BAGS

IS NOT LINCOLN CENTER WHERE IT BELONGS?

ASSEMBLE TO COLLECT GARBAGE → 5 PM FEBRUARY 12 at ↓
THEN MARCH TO LINCOLN CENTER (9th Street between C and D)
BE AT LINCOLN CENTER BY 8:30 PM FOR THE GARBAGE PLANTING CEREMONY

UP AGAINST THE WALL MOTHER*FUCKER - and into the trashcan

DAY FOUR

On the subject of art and activism, I wanted to ask about the action at Lincoln Center, when you dumped the garbage in the fountain: isn't there an artistic idea behind it? Is that a kind of art?

It is. It's guerrilla theater. A lot of people who were with us, at that point, came from what they used to call guerrilla theater. They were theater people, and people interested in a kind of street performance. A lot of them gravitated toward Black Mask. So they were part of the beginning of Up Against the Wall. Most of them didn't stay with it, it became too militant. But they were part of the beginning, and that's when we dumped the garbage at Lincoln Center.

Really a lot of those actions were theatrical. Like shutting down MOMA, or getting the free night at the Fillmore. Even the occupation at Columbia, and the breakaways, to some extent. In a sense all actions are performative, so there's some element of theater.

And that was an important influence. There was this element within us that wasn't purely political, that was artistic, theatrical, poetic. We couldn't have done what we did, if it was only political people.

When you say it became too militant: where does it cross the line, where it's no longer theater? For example storming the Pentagon is very militant, in the sense that the risk is big.

We thought we could get shot!

It's more of a serious risk, and also there's more contingency. It can't be scripted beforehand, like you don't know how many people will join...

And you don't know what the response will be. They could shoot! It happened, at Kent State. But that didn't enter into our decision. We'd decided what we were going to do. Whether we lived or died was not the issue.

Because the objective was to stop the war. To stop the US war machine itself.

To stop the Vietnam War, correct. We didn't do it under the illusion that we would be victorious. We did it with the feeling that we must try.

But to risk your life, you must have believed that something was possible. You were doing it for a reason.

The Vietnam War made a big impact on us as a generation. We felt that this war of oppression was being carried out, in a sense, in our name. And we felt that that war had to be ended. Even if it meant losing our lives in the effort.

It was also connected to the Black struggle. The civil rights movement had become extremely militant, you had SNCC, you had the Panthers. We felt like we were part of that move toward a radical change. It might sound strange, but we believed that a revolution in America was possible. We actually believed it could happen in our time. We felt like, "now is our chance."

Including armed struggle.

At some point, we realized that if the effort wasn't militant enough, and complete enough, we would end up with just a slight change. A liberal veneer. And we were influenced really strongly by Black militants, people like Robert Williams, who wrote *Negroes with Guns.* We were close with the Panthers. I was friendly with Rap Brown. We gravitated toward the most militant end of the Black struggle.

A lot of people were not ready for that. When we started, it was such a minority that saw the need for an extreme militant response. But slowly that was growing.

Around you there were people that shared this feeling, like friends and comrades that were equally intensified?

Yes. And those few created energy that pulled a few more. And then that pulled a few more, and so on. It kept growing. But in the beginning it was just a few. Just a handful.

Important question: to create energy, to inspire people with your energy, in other words means that the energy must run through your action?

Correct. Propaganda of the deed.

And you did it through militant action, and also community building.

And excitement. And actually, even art. Like we got guerrilla theater people involved. They weren't activists. But they had a certain poetic way of doing things that attracted attention. We didn't say “oh well they’re just theater people.” We said “okay, we need them. Let’s do something more theatrical, that also has a political message.” And we created an energy, just a handful of us. It’s hard to believe…we spread it all over the country! Everywhere people were emulating it.

What’s outstanding to me about what you did, is that this theatrical artistic element, and this militant element were together.

Exactly.

That doesn’t happen so much. It tends to be split. Like artists just do peace through art, you know.

For us, they were not separate. They worked together. They needed each other.

I can see why art needs militancy. But why did the militancy need art?

Because there was little already existing. So in order to build something, it was necessary to create excitement and energy. You couldn’t do it with just ideology.

That’s why I always compare two events that we were involved in: cutting the fences at Woodstock, and breaking into the Pentagon. They’re so different, but that’s why I like to use that example. To emphasize that, to me, they were both important. Most political people can’t understand it. To them it’s like “who cares about a rock concert?” But to me, cutting the fences at Woodstock and making it a free event, was also important. I mean, 500,000 people free! It showed that people didn’t need producers: they needed each other.

In other words, there was no hierarchy. It’s not like the political was more important than the cultural. They’re both essential. And that to me has always been the hallmark of who we were. We didn't have a hierarchy.

Maybe this is too simple, but it's like you were thinking about the act itself, and the happening. Rather than weighing and measuring the effect.

Or they both carried some essential element that needed to be understood. Or like we had the Fillmore East free one day a week. We put on free concerts for people in the community. The political people thought "well that's not political." How could you be more political than to say, "be free!" You can't commodify life! See, they create those definitions that limit political understanding.

It's controlled by the logic of the State, if you follow this divide. To think that only attacking the Pentagon is important, and culture is just secondary.

And nobody in the political world understood that they were both important.

Did you have a lot of debates?

No, you could just tell. Like to them it's just a bunch of dope smoking hippies, who cares. They're more worried about the proletariat. But where in the hell do you think those kids came from?

Marxists are more concerned with the unification of proletarians for revolution, or something like that. But you had a different idea of revolution.

It was more cultural than purely political. It was an effort to change life. The quality of life. The way you lived and how to live — that was important. It wasn't about control.

But there were some other political groups that tried to engage the counterculture, right? Like the Yippies, wasn't their project a little similar?

But with a big difference. Abbie Hoffman, Jerry Rubin, all those guys were media freaks. They were obsessed with the media. And they became fixated on their own image. I was the opposite. I avoided visibility. Like I would never allow myself to be photographed.

It's true, I've hardly ever seen a picture of you.

I didn't want to be a personality. And that might seem like a small thing, but Abbie and those guys did the opposite. Whenever they saw a camera, they would run to it. And they were co-opted so fast.

To resist cooptation, you strategically avoided the media?

Yes. On some level it's just obvious, you know, they wanted to be stars. You must understand that cooptation would follow. Or like our name: you couldn't print the word "motherfucker," at that time. So the regular media couldn't write about us. We didn't choose it as a name for that reason. But thanks to that we were less likely to be co-opted.

Did the Yippies ever participate in what you were doing, though? They were part of that group levitating the Pentagon, that drew a lot of attention.

They weren't enemies. They weren't allies. We had different aims. For us, it wasn't a media campaign. We were there to resist.

More than the image, it was about the act.

And it was the effort. We wanted to make an effort to stop the war in

Vietnam. Not to protest or appeal, but to make a real effort to stop it. And to show that some people in America will fight to end this war.

It's not that I think everyone could be a militant. And even in the '60s, you could see that in order to change America, to really bring it down, it was going to take more than just the militants. That was apparent then, it's even more clear now. We need people in all strata of society. It's not possible with just militants.

That's something refreshing about you. You don't glorify militancy. You don't brag like "back then we were more revolutionary."

I do the opposite. I tell young people, "you may not do what we did in the '60s." Can you imagine trying to enter the Pentagon? It'd be crazy to advise someone to do it. In the '60s we chose a way forward, a way that may not be retraced in exactly the same way. Circumstances have changed tremendously. We must therefore understand how to get around them. The question that matters is to find the way forward today.

But what's interesting in terms of history, your trajectory was very unique. You were a small group of armed militants. But unlike many others, you had no authoritarian structure. And you never became vanguardist. That happened with the Weathermen, right?

They were Leninists. And that's where we disagreed. You know, they used to hang around with us. Before they were Weathermen. They were college students. And they used to come and hang around our crash pads. Some of them became more militant by being around us. Then they went in this Leninist direction that we didn't agree with. I saw it happen.

In other words, at first you were militant together in terms of action?

Correct.

But then they became more vanguardist in terms of ideas, they became Leninist. And they became isolated, their conduct became more and more based in the small group.

Right. But that had other historical precedents also. I mean there were anarchist bands like that, there were guerrilla groups. There were a large variety of directions. And I can't say that they shouldn't have done what they did — that's up to them. But we chose a different path.

Your way of using arms seems different too. A lot of armed groups are thinking about confrontation with the State, and they become embroiled in that. But for you, it was more for self-defense maybe, like protecting people in the Lower East Side.

It was both.

Sometimes you used them to advance the greater causes as well, like isn't there a story about getting the Fillmore East free night, and threatening Bill Graham?

Well, I didn't threaten him…

Wasn't there some story about three bullets?

But it wasn't a threat. I never threatened anyone. I just told him how it was gonna be! What happened was, when we approached Bill Graham about having the theater free one night a week, at first he refused. During a meeting in his office, he took out three silver bullets and put them on his desk. He said "these were given to me by the Hell's Angels, because they wanted something from me. And now you want something from me." I said "yes, the only difference is, if we give you three bullets they're not gonna be on your desk. We want the theater one night free for the community."

Yeah, that sounds convincing. You guys were intense!

We were like the psychedelic mafia!

This might be a tricky question. But to confront the State, means you confront the force of its military. And at some point you can't survive that. So then, is there a limit to militancy? Or how do you navigate that limit?

But that's a false question, in a sense. Each person must decide what their limit is. I can't decide for others.

But I mean as a historical problem. For example in the Chinese Revolution, the communists became a military. To fight against the Japanese military they became a military themselves. But you wouldn't become a military, right?

Right, I wouldn't suggest anything like that. But it's not only ideological — it's also emotional. So how you're going to respond to something, you must determine when it happens.

Emotional, that's interesting. That's really true. When I look at the history of the Chinese Red Army, they were fighting against Japanese imperialism, while also trying to quell Chinese fascist groups. And you know, I think I'm an anarchist but I can't say exactly how I would have responded.

And if I was in Cuba, I probably would have gone into the mountains with the guerrillas. But I would resist their becoming a military. And there were anarchists and extreme Left people there as well.

That's why, to me, there are no ideological boundaries. You may have a code, that certain things you wouldn't do. But whether or not you do them is an individual decision, it can't be predetermined ideologically. It's determined in each instance. There's no line out there that says "okay I'll go so far, but I won't cross this line."

It's up to each person to see the boundaries as they go. Yet always remaining non-authoritarian.

DAY FIVE

Today we're hoping to talk more about how you operated back in the day. You said you never tried to organize?

I never even organized my life! We never organized anything. We just lived.

You didn't try to organize other people to do something. You just did things together, like with friends or whoever came along.

I'll show you an example. It's a classic example I always think of. One night we were sitting around, and a bunch of the women in the family walked in, all dressed up. They had a certain way of dressing, you know, they had an exotic style. And on this occasion it was like, "shit man, where are you guys going?" They said "the chief of police is speaking, so we're gonna go drive him off the stage. You guys can come watch us, or you can stay home and cook dinner. See you later!" That's how we worked. They didn't say "what do you think, should we do it?" They were like, "this is what we're doing. You could come watch, or you could stay home."

So we went. And we thought if the police really interfere, we'll be there. But they didn't ask us for that. And they drove the chief of police off the stage! Captain Fink.

So it was based on autonomous, spontaneous action. Rather than coordinating the whole group.

We never had a meeting! Our family, our group, never had an official meeting. We talked to each other. Like you're eating dinner, you discuss things. But we never said "okay let's have a meeting."

And you didn't try to mobilize people, like try to get a hundred people to do something. You just did it, and some people joined and some didn't. Is that how you worked?

Pretty much. But once in a while, like I was thinking about the event where we stormed the Pentagon — that may be the closest we ever came to organizing. We went around to different groups and told them our idea that we wanted to all be in the same place. So if it looked like we could do something more radical, we would be together. So in a way that was somewhat organizational. But it wasn't organizational in the sense that we asked people to sign on.

It wasn't a command.

We didn't even ask "will you do it?" We just suggested. It wasn't like we would go to SDS and talk to the front office, and they'd say "okay we'll endorse it." We just told people what we thought, that we wanted to meet in a certain area. If you show up, good. If you don't, whatever. There was no effort to get them to agree.

But you did go to SDS meetings, like some national and regional conferences. Technically weren't you even a member group?

We were the only non-student chapter. One time we ran for office! When the candidates went to make their speeches, one of us went up with a wastepaper basket on his head and said "I nominate this wastepaper basket!" Our position was to throw all the position papers away.

It's not about participating in the organization, more like disrupting it.

And showing that there were other ways to be. We felt that it was important to inject humor into the struggle, not just militancy.

By many accounts I've read, it does seem that you had a radicalizing effect on SDS.

But it's not that we were organizing students. Like different Marxist groups were always arguing about the role of students in the revolution, and how to organize the workers with the students. To us, the most revolutionary thing a student could do was to stop being a student!

Because some Marxists envision unification of one movement, under the party, as revolution. But you believe more in a kind of free association, and mutual empowerment?

I believed everybody was necessary to bring it about. But they didn't have to agree, or be unified. There was no central committee. I'm totally opposed to the idea of a central committee. It becomes authoritarian, it feeds control.

Some people might not like me saying this, but to me, that's what Marxism is: it's an ideology of control. It seeks to replace the centralized control of the capitalist, with centralized socialist control. I mean "the dictatorship of the proletariat:" how could you propose a revolution based on a group that's talking about dictatorship, of anything? The minute they say "dictatorship," you have to say "oh shit, I'm not going in that direction!"

Because such a thing as the proletariat doesn't exist, it's a concept.

Even if it existed, you don't want a dictatorship. The revolutionary effort is to destroy power. Not to become it, or take it over, or replace it with your own.

And you know, you can't just blame Stalin. The Left wants to put the blame on Stalin. But Stalin is a descendent of Lenin. It's a worse extreme, but it is a direct descendent. And in a way, Lenin is a descendant of Marx. So you have to see the connection. If you look at Marx himself, and his involvement with the International, you could see that he was authoritarian. He wanted to dictate who could belong to the International. They had the anarchists kicked out, they had Bakunin expelled. So people should have realized then, that that's a future problem. It was there way back in the beginning.

And then it becomes all socialists or social democrats, and they start discussing some bullshit argument like workers should go to war for their nations. And tacitly embracing State power. That's because the anarchists were gone.

The Marxists got rid of them! And they moved to Switzerland. You know that's where the theory of anarchism was formulated, in the Jura. French Switzerland. But so the problem with Marxism grew from there, it started in the First International.

Another problem with the concept of the proletariat, like the classic Marxist reading heralds the industrial proletariat, right? But in the same move it ignores farmers, peasants, women, Indigenous people, and so on.

It's because a lot of Marxists, including Marx, were obsessed with the means of production. So they emphasized the industrial worker. And they despised the lumpen. They created that as a derogatory term. But the lumpen were more revolutionary, in a way. Actually, I gravitated toward the lumpen.

I agree with you. The lumpen are more our comrades, like the underclass that's against the law, and anti-work.

And we understood that in the '60s, we saw that the revolution was not coming from the factory, but from the street, from Black America, from the youth, from all these marginalized groups. So we celebrated that.

Your style was very different from other Leftist groups at the time.

Totally different. We didn't even think of ourselves as Left. We were a combination of radical consciousness, and New Age consciousness. We felt we reflected both.

Like a new cultural movement, or something like that?

It was a youth movement. Not labor movement.

And it wasn't just America but around the world – you had the sense that it was happening everywhere?

It *was* happening everywhere. The more we understood it, the more excited we became. And we saw that there were more people thinking this way, it wasn't just us. There were different groups around the world, like the Provos, even the Situationists to a degree, all trying to understand how this new energy could be manifest. It wasn't the traditional Left.

What was your relation to the Situationists?

We corresponded for a while. They never asked me to join. We just communicated back and forth, sharing ideas. And then they expelled me. I told them, "you can't expel me. I'm not a member!"

Why did they try to expel you?

Two reasons. One was that some people thought I was too activist and less theoretical. Then some people felt that some people in my family were too mystical.

What does that mean?

I don't know. I never asked them. What happened was that Guy Debord sent Raoul Vaneigem to see me. So he came to see me. And when he came I wasn't there, I was gone for the afternoon, or maybe I was out for the hour. But anyway he came and he met one of my cohorts. He was the most poetic, quote unquote "mystical" element in the family. Well to me that didn't mean anything, you know, I wasn't opposed. But when Vaneigem talked with him, I guess he decided that he was too mystical. Which meant that I must be too mystical. He never talked to me. Then I got a letter from Debord saying that they expelled me.

I still don't understand the critique. Also being too activist, what was that about?

The problem with the Situationists was that they were too ideological. To be a Situationist, meant to think like a Situationist. You can't think independently. You have to think alike. And I didn't agree with that theoretical dictate. But Guy Debord was a total egotist. You had to think like him.

Eventually Debord kicked everyone out.

If he could have, he would have kicked himself out! In fact, he did.
You know, a lot of these militants and Leftists have a scholastic

background. And they talk as if the words they use are real. Whereas we didn't care to discuss ideology, like "you think this, I think that." We never had a meeting to discuss ideology. And a lot of people in the family had no defined ideology. I can't even say that everyone was an anarchist. I don't know what they were. We were wild. Not definable. And we thrived on it.

You did associate with a lot of anarchists, weren't you close with Murray Bookchin?

I knew Murray really well. He was like an uncle. I always used to tease him, "Murray you're not an anarchist. You're a Trotskyist in anarchist clothing!" And it used to piss him off! But that was the truth. He was more of a Trotskyist than an anarchist.

Ideologically, he might have been an anarchist. He had the theory of anarchism down. But if you spent time with him you knew, his demeanor, his approach, his way of thinking, his way of talking — everything was Trotskyist, only leaning toward anarchist. That's what he came out of. It was ingrained in him. I'm not being negative.

In books things are different. But in living, there's a side to anarchism that defies definition. You act it out. It's not an ideology, it's a way of living. Murray was an anarchist by definition. I was an anarchist in living.

You were introduced to anarchism from Murray though?

No, not at all. The Living Theater were probably the first people that I associated with who were anarchist. That was way before Murray. I actually started with the Living Theater when I was 17. They were phenomenal. At that time, I knew my philosophical and political inclination was anarchist. But I never used the term "anarchist," I was not aware of that term. And they put the name to how I really was. So I started using that word after. They were pacifist anarchists, which I never was. But I was really close to them, Julian Beck and Judith Malina. They really meant a lot to me.

You said the family never had a meeting. But how did you come together in the first place? I mean how did you find each other?

We weren't an organization, you couldn't join. Like if somebody would come around and say "can I join Up Against the Wall?" No, there's nothing to join! And see that's what saved us. We were never infiltrated, because you couldn't join. So that meant you had to come and be around us, and live with us. And we get to know you on some other basis.

Like everyday life. You become a living partner. It's not a membership.

Exactly. And then we had different affinity groups, like there was one group that was more students, and college drop-outs, you know, intellectual. Then there was the street group. Then there was the heavy-duty group.

There was no central organization, but a constellation of small groups.

The theory of an affinity group is that you have something in common that you want to do. But you don't tell other people about it. You just do it. And there's some things that we did, that you couldn't tell other people. So that was the theory, like nobody has to know! I mean we never had a meeting, or took a vote. Not once.

And they overlapped. They liked each other, they did certain things together. For instance when we occupied Columbia University, it was all of us, the student group, the street group… We booby-trapped a whole building!

The Math Building?

Correct. And we set traps — the police were starting to invade the buildings that were held, and they were beating people. We told them "hey we're waiting, come evict us." And they wouldn't come in the building. They negotiated for us to leave. After the other buildings had all been evicted, we negotiated our withdrawal.

The student group, I remember you said that one of the crash pads had more students: were they also part of SDS? They were connected with Columbia students?

Yes. They were part of Columbia SDS. And they were more Marxist, but they liked our style. So they started to become more like us.

Because you share this lifestyle of a crash pad, that's beyond political ideology. So even Marxists, it's okay you can work together. You trust them.

And we would interact, you know, we did things together. Sometimes I'd stay at their crash pad and we would hang out. I became really close with some of them.

Right. So they're not just students at Columbia. They live with you in the Lower East Side. So you share something beyond ideology. The everyday living becomes the basis for affinity.

And that was our strength. That we had all these different levels of activity, levels of thinking, of being. Like it was intellectual, it was activist, it was street...It wasn't that you had to be a certain way, to be part of the group. The extreme opposite would be the Situationists, where everyone had to think alike.

So we had our core group, there were street people that came and joined it, there were theater people, and poets, there were students. There were old anarchists that came with us, that had fought in Spain with Durruti. We had others that were ex-military,

Vietnam vets. Then the young people and runaways that came with us. All these different elements mixed and interacted.

You know this concept "form of life?" I feel like what you're talking about is not sharing the same form of life, but a multiplicity of forms of life interacting in a way that's empowering.

And we were comfortable with everybody being who they were. If we wanted everyone to be alike, we could not have existed as we did. I made it clear that you don't have to be like me. We have something to do, let's do it. You could be any way you were. It's not ideological. And it's not long-lasting, you may not stay together forever. You may stay together for a year, and do something. We had no sense that "well we're building a movement." We just moved!

It makes me think about ideology as an emotional response. It wants to realize change in a certain way. But it's also a discomfort with things changing, and the unknown.

And to be honest with you, it's hard to separate the reality of how we did things from personality. I was one kind of person. I don't know how it would have happened if I was a different person.

It's not like great actions and achievements gather around ideologies. But particular arrangements of personality create some weird power.

And it might just be momentary. But that's how nature is. Lightning! It doesn't last forever. And in reality, a year together is eternity, in a sense. Or it's less than a second in the scale of the universe. Time is relative.

It's not like the longer duration, the better. There's no objective measure.

You know, my idea was always "something has to be done." We're not trying to build a movement forever, we're trying to accomplish something. Because something has to be done. Life has to be changed. And I don't know what the future holds.

It's like the cliched political question, "what is to be done?" There's some paradox. When you feel absolutely that something has to be done, there is no question. But when you're debating the question of what should be done, the feeling itself can get lost.

And the conception of the time you need: that could be the mistake. You need energy, correct. But it's ongoing. It's perpetual. It is movement.

UP AGAINST THE WALL MOTHERFUCKERS
I
W W
C

DAY SIX

Ben, the other day I overheard you say something I wanted to ask about. You were talking about Native American Plains cultures and their affinity with anarchism. Would you say more about that?

Sure, I could give an example. Most Western people have no idea, like there's the stereotypical image of the chief, right? Well in reality, in a lot of Plains cultures, the chief is not an authority. He's a figurehead. He plays a role ceremonially, he plays a role in society. But he's not in charge. They choose people that they have respect for, to be a figurehead. It's a really intelligent way to do things. You have a figurehead that has no authority. That's really anarchist!

So the decision making process also, it's not just up to the chief to decide.

No. The headmen, the clans get together and they decide.

You also talked about it in terms of geography and being nomadic, and the social formations that were possible in the

Plains. Like if a group couldn't reach agreement sometimes they would just split, instead of trying to control each other.

Yeah like for instance, there's one Plains tribe called Shoshone. They had a split, and one group moved entirely to a different part of the Plains. But America is a big place, so they could do that. They moved from Wyoming all the way down to Texas, basically on the border of Mexico, that's how far they went. And those people that went south, they became Comanches, they became a very dominant tribe. They had a lot of horses, you know, the tribes that had the closest relation with horses became dominant tribes in the Plains.

But it's a different kind of domination, not in today's sense.

It's not dominance in the capitalist sense. It's dominance in the sense that they have a larger territory that they're using and so they can keep you away. They don't own more, but they use more. They could spread their dominion further. They didn't say "we own this." Native cultures don't believe in owning the land. But they used it. So they would clash, if one tribe encroached on the territory that another tribe was using, they would fight. The warriors would fight. They weren't out to exterminate each other, just to stop them from encroaching. And tribes would move, maybe there were too many conflicts so they would give up the land they were on and move to another area, and then they would defend that new area. They didn't own it, they set claim that they were using it.

And a lot of Plains tribes were nomadic right, so there was a culture of moving.

Some moved all the time. You know, what you see when you think of Plains cultures, a lot of that started two or three hundred years ago, when the horses came. The Spanish brought horses. And as different tribes started getting horses, they were able to move out further into the Plains.

In other words, after they're already fighting against the Western colonizers.

Right. Like for instance the white colonizer, the French and the British, pushed Native people into the Plains. So tribes also started fighting each other, to find a territory. But they were pushed. And they went deeper into the Plains because they had horses. And the buffalo were in the Plains.

For example there were some tribes around the Great Lakes that did farming, and at certain times of year they would move into the Plains to hunt buffalo. But the Plains are vast, and they didn't have horses yet. So they would only go so far, and they'd come back for the winter. Well eventually, some other tribes in Canada got guns from the French and the British, and they started forcing these Great Lakes tribes out, which didn't have guns. But as they were forced out, going south, they also acquired horses, which were coming north from Mexico. They developed a horse culture, and they moved deeper into the Plains. In other words, as some tribes got guns, others found horses, and they were able to stay out in the Plains.

That's a vivid illustration of how colonization changed the terms of war.

But it wasn't war like the colonizers' war. You could use the word "skirmish" instead of war. They were warriors, and they had skirmishes. In a lot of Plains tribes, to hit an enemy without killing him was a sign of bravery. Because you went that close, and faced death, that was more honorable. They called it counting coup. They had what's called a coup stick, you see it in pictures sometimes, it's got a crook. They used to ride with it. In other words, it wasn't like a world war that kills a hundred thousand people. They weren't out to exterminate each other. It was a more human form of warfare.

But people don't understand nature. Like when people talk about being anti-war, I always say, you know, I'm not opposed to war. I am opposed to wars of extermination. But war is a reality.

Our bodies are at war every moment! The white blood cells are fighting, the viruses are being attacked. War is not bad: it's necessary. It's oppression that is bad. But war is a natural phenomenon.

Even when I was an activist against the Vietnam War, I never became "anti-war." I was against the Vietnam War, because it was a war of extermination and a war of occupation. The Vietnamese should have a right to self-determination. The US should stay the hell out of there. But that's not anti-war.

You're not a pacifist. You're a militant.

And also, it's like we were talking about the other day, that's what's wrong with being politically correct. There's no nuance. If you just say "well I'm anti-war," what does that mean? Does it include wars of liberation?

For instance say the conflict now in Armenia and Azerbaijan. Relatively speaking, you have to be able to understand which is closer to your end. And to me, autonomy is more essential. I support the autonomy of people in that region. They want to be autonomous, so they should. It's not a matter of being pro-Armenia or anti-Azerbaijan, it's that I'm pro-autonomy and in this case Armenia is more for autonomy than Azerbaijan. In another case it might be different. That's why relativity is important, because you're able to decide in each instance.

Like you said, you will fight with Black nationalists against the American government. But you're not agreeing with nationalism. I wonder if this is why you were able to form relationships with so many different groups, across ideological lines. For example you sometimes worked with the Black Panthers?

That's where relativity comes in. In terms of the struggle against the white supremacist establishment, I'm with the Panthers. But in conjunction with another struggle, I might be opposed to the

Panthers in favor of a more autonomous group. In other words, I'm not for the Panthers all the time. For instance in the Black struggle, there were independent movements that were more locally based, more community-based, and they allowed for more autonomy in each group. The Panthers were a national organization, they had a certain influence.

They tried to create a party, right?

Right. But then also within the Panthers, there were huge differences. So that's relativity: in a particular instance, which one represents your view more? It's not that one is right or wrong, but one is closer to what you seek.

Generally speaking, it seems like you had good relations with the Panthers.

They liked us because we weren't there only to support them. Other political groups were professing to support the Black struggle. We didn't believe in that. We weren't doing it just to support them. We were fighting alongside them. We had a common enemy.

There was a man named James Carr, he was a Black Panther. He wrote a book called *Bad*. And in the afterword, it's referenced that Bobby Seale had talked about appointing me as an honorary member of the Panthers. Well that was the reason. Because I wasn't there only to support them. We were not supporting their struggle. We were allied in struggle.

Were you engaged in the Newark or Harlem riots, or you knew people involved?

Yeah like during the Harlem riots, H. Rap Brown called me. He said "don't come up here, do something down there that's gonna pull police away from here." And I agreed, I said "that's right, that's exactly what I'm trying to do." So we did something in the streets in the Lower East Side. There were cops ringing it, there were snipers on the roof— which meant that those forces couldn't be in Harlem.

How did other radicals deal with the Harlem riots, like Bookchin and his group for example, did they get involved?

No, Bookchin sympathized with the Black struggle, but it wasn't part of his life. He was really focused on the larger environmental, ecological problem. And actually, I feel that each group has to find their place. And Bookchin had a place. For him to go to Harlem would be like me going to China. He sympathized, but he had nothing to do with them.

Or use an example like Greta Thunberg. She's doing something, she doesn't have to be part of Black Lives Matter, for example. I'm sure she's sympathetic toward it. But she doesn't have to join that struggle. She's doing something else that's valuable. We need all of that.

That's another problem with being politically correct, everybody has to fit in the same framework. You know Valerie Solanas? We were friends. She was very critical of the liberal feminist movement for that reason. Like how shallow, how one-dimensional...She always used to make fun it. To her it was a middle-class plaything. Like, we want to change the reality! Not change titles or status.

Valerie Solanas shot Andy Warhol right? You were close with her before that?

Very close. She used to stay with me. Like now, the bell might ring, and she'd say "it's Valerie, I don't have any place to stay tonight." And I'd say "come on up, stay on the couch." She would stay with me sometimes days on end. We were just friends, you know, we were buddies. But we were very close.

A week before she shot Andy, she came to see me. It was during the Columbia occupation. I don't know how she found me, or how she got in the building. But she came and asked me, "what would happen if I shot someone?" I said "it depends on two things: who you shoot, and whether they die or not." She said "okay," and went off. One week later she shot Andy. I didn't see her again after that.

You supported her shooting of Andy?

I did. I was the only one! I made a leaflet in her support. After she shot Andy, the next day I went uptown and handed it out. That was one of my favorite pieces I ever wrote.

Will you tell us about what happened, and why you supported her?

You know, Valerie was a beautiful person. And she was a little unbalanced, which never bothered me. It still doesn't. She had an edge to her. We were similar in many ways. We shared a lot. I mean I was really close to her. And I couldn't stand Andy. I had a strong animosity towards him and that whole bunch. Politically, aesthetically, on every level. As a person he was really despicable as well, and that's why Valerie hated him. He used and manipulated people. Then another trigger was that Andy took her screenplay. I don't know if he really stole it, or how that evolved. In her mind, she was fixated with the thought that he had stolen it. And when she tried to approach him about it he just pushed her off. But Valerie was the wrong person to mess with.

You knew Andy Warhol too?

I never had a personal relation, but he was around, you know. He was the most manipulative, self-centered, money-hungry...I mean he was a sick person.

Also as an artist, you were critical of his art.

Totally. I feel that creativity is a profound, even spiritual act. Warhol was the exact opposite. He used art as a commodity. He tried to deny and purge the core of creativity, and put it on a commercial basis.

You know, it's almost egotistical for me to say this, but art plays a really important role in the world. From the cave paintings forward, or even before, art has been an essential part of human life. It's an attempt to move forward. To break. But with commercialization, it went backwards. It went from being a vital experiment, to just another commercial entity. And so Pop Art played a bigger role in repression than people recognize. In a way it signaled that the commercial world was going to win. And it has won — but only for the moment.

You were actually there on the frontlines, fighting against it.

And in all these years, I never gave up art. I would not enter the commercial art world. I've stayed out of it for sixty years. But art is a need. I always say that art is like breathing.

Warhol started his Factory in the '60s, on Union Square right? So you would run into those people, or like the Velvet Underground, were they around the Lower East Side?

Yeah they were around St. Mark's, Electric Circus. The Velvet Underground performed in the Lower East Side.

Were you friends with the Velvet Underground? No. You were friends with Canned Heat, right? Would you talk about the difference, why you liked Canned Heat and not Velvet Underground?

I don't know how to put it in words, but it's aesthetic. Velvet Underground was middle-class bullshit music. Bourgeois entertainment. Canned Heat was real. They were part of an energy that we shared. So you're listening to them, but they're not entertaining you, they're sharing. The Velvet Underground was part of that commercial world of entertainment.

You know this guy today that makes those balloon figures, Jeff Koons? I was talking with somebody the other day and I said, "compared to Jeff Koons, Andy Warhol was Rembrandt!" See, that's also relativity.

But Jeff Koons is related to Warhol, no? I mean they're in a similar line.

Oh totally. He's Warhol on steroids.

But if we look at it from your perspective in the '60s, it's like you were anticipating it, this total permeation of commercialism.

Right. I could see it coming!

You left New York in '69, and stayed away for many decades. Were you shocked to see the change when you came back?

Not so much surprised as disheartened. To see that in some ways it didn't progress at all, and in some ways it got worse. It didn't get better.

Can you say more about the differences between the '60s and today?

Everything is more commodified, and centralized. In the '60s, bad as it was, there were more possibilities. Like back then the police were just local beat walkers. They were overweight, not heavily armed, they didn't have a clue what was coming down. We were actually better armed, and in better shape than them. Now the police are totally militarized.

But at the same time, the resistance is bigger today. Which is also a qualitative difference. Could you imagine in the '60s that Black Lives Matter would have millions of people in the street? So now the numbers are more in our favor, but the oppression is stronger and more dangerous.

And the progressives, I don't think they understand America. They're still trying to move toward socialism, but that word is anathema, it's attached to centralization. If you could bring those ideas out in a non-authoritarian way, you might have a better chance to attract people.

Actually, I feel that the concept of Left versus Right has become outdated. Obviously between the two, I'm more sympathetic to the Left. But was Stalin Left? Were Lenin and Trotsky Left, when they wiped out the anarchists? That's why, to me, it's more important to differentiate between authoritarian and non-authoritarian.

I've been thinking about the word "freedom." It's overloaded in the American context, now it's mainly used by the right wing. But the way you talk about it really resonates, like when you say you wanted to live free. It evokes the liberatory impetus of the '60s. I feel like no one talks about freedom like that anymore.

They forgot! They forgot what it's all about. See I'm really part of the '60s. I'm a political animal, but I'm a '60s version. And to us, the sense of freedom overrode ideology. It was just to be free! That was what we were doing. We wanted to be free in our mind. In our body, in our culture.

That's what's interesting, it's this collective sensibility, and it's also embodied. It seems specific to American history, for example there's no parallel in Japan. It's somewhat an American phenomenon, would you say?

I wouldn't say that it's exclusively American. But the sense of personal freedom is definitely a strong current. Like with Emma Goldman and that generation of anarchists, there was a sense of personal freedom that was not for sale. We came from that more than we came from the European May Day, which had an organizational impetus. For us, the vehicle to freedom was not organizational — it was anti-organizational!

It's like the saying, "if I can't dance to it, it's not my revolution." That's a metaphor for that sense of freedom. It may be a romanticized way of expressing it, but we were motivated by that sense. We were part of that history.

Valerie Lives

Andy Warhol shot by Valerie Solonas. Plastic Man vs. the Sweet Assassin–the face of plastic/fascist smashed–the terrorist knows where to strike–at the heart–a red plastic inevitable exploded–non-man shot by the reality of his dream (as the cultural assassin emerges–a touch chick with a bop cap and a 38–the true vengence of DADA–touch little chick–the "hater" of men and the lover of man–with the surgeon's gun–NOW–against the wall of plastic extinction–an epoxy nightmare with a dead superstar–the statue of liberty raped by a chick with balls–the camp master slain by the slave–and America's white plastic cathedral is ready to burn. VALERIE IS OURS AND THE SWEET ASSASSIN LIVES.

UPAGAINST THE WALL
MOTHERFUCKER
S.C.U.M. in exile

DAY SEVEN

I have a question about the late '60s, when the anti-Vietnam War movement, student activism, and Black liberation were all energized and strong. At some point, did you feel that there was a chance – I don't know if I should use the word "revolution," but you felt it may really be possible to remove the government, or decompose the power, you had some hopeful vision like that?

If I understand the question correctly, yes, I thought it was possible. I believed it. I mean I couldn't have done what I did if I didn't believe it. If I thought it was futile, would I have put my life on the line? We were moving in a way that felt like, "it is now, this could happen." I had to believe it.

I'm also curious about the moment when you had that belief, but then you lost it.

I didn't lose the belief that it was possible. I lost the belief that it would happen today. In the '60s the appeal was that we can change it, now. I woke up every day and felt like "we're gonna do it." We're gonna bring it down. Or die trying.

But at some point I realized that it wasn't going to happen immediately. The powers that be had been able to stop it. They had retaken the front, or the beachhead, so to speak. I could see that the chance of us bringing about the change was gone. But only for that moment.

That's what I'm curious about. Because it happened so fast, one year there's imminent possibility, the next it's gone. It must have been so intense to live through that.

And I don't know how we knew it, but somehow you could feel that this was our chance. It was the crucial moment. But the conservative world crushed it. They pushed back, it happened all over the world. And it's gotten worse ever since. What we were afraid of then, actually happened. But you could feel that we were close to having success at changing something.

You kind of saw it coming already? Like more intense capitalism, commodification, environmental destruction, all of that?

In every realm. It was the beginning of the counterrevolution. It's lasted up until now. But we could see it then. That was part of the reason for leaving. A lot of us went out west. At some point we realized that the powers that be had retaken control. And we began to understand that in order to have an alternative world, we had to build it. We reached that point in '69. It took most people into the '70s.

So there was a sense of leaving together? Not that people just individually scattered.

Correct. It wasn't that we gave up the fight. But to continue the fight, and grow stronger. We saw the chance to leave urban existence behind, and start to build new ways of living. Many people reached a similar point, like the Back to the Land movement was starting. We had a parallel development in a sense.

Can you say more about what was happening, how you knew. Because the struggle in '69 still appeared vibrant, in many aspects. How did you realize when you did?

Well I had certain signals. Because it was a matter of survival. Even if I felt the revolution could still happen, I myself faced elimination.For instance, I was going to the Chicago protests, I was traveling with my girlfriend. She had a blue Volkswagen that I frequently used to travel in. Along the way we were stopping different places, Detroit, Ann Arbor, wherever we had friends. And I got a call from Chicago. Someone called to warn me that the cops were stopping blue Volkswagens, and they had my picture. They approached the car with guns drawn, like they were expecting a standoff. Or they were going to provoke one. Later on I got another call, saying the same thing. Then a third call, the same. At that point I turned around.

Meaning, the Feds were really after you. You'd been marked.

So it was both. On a personal level I'd reached a stalemate. But I could see that the movement had also reached a stalemate.

So after what happened in Chicago, you decided to leave and go out west?

No. That wasn't fully understood, or planned at that point. But once we realized we were going to leave, we moved a lot of the younger runaways out of the city. We took them to San Francisco, where we thought they'd be safer. I felt like I couldn't leave them behind. It was something I had to do before leaving.

But to get the kids across the country, see we couldn't use any of our cars, you know, because they'd be followed. But we managed to steal a credit card. Back then, credit cards were rare. And it wasn't as easy to disable them. So it was a big deal. We used it to rent cars, and get gas and food, the whole trip. We would change cars every so often to avoid being followed. In the end we used five different cars! The last one went into the Pacific.

Really? That's incredible. I never heard that story.

Oh there's so much that I never…It's never come up. I remember one moment, we were driving across the country, and we stopped at a mall to get supplies. So we asked the kids what they wanted. You know we had this credit card, we could get whatever they wanted. And they all said that they didn't want anything.

That's beautiful.

A true non-commodity reality.

What happened with the kids, did they stay together for a while?

They stayed together at the beginning. But I lost track, you know, because I went into the wilderness. I never followed the progression.

You didn't keep in touch, even years later?

Well I cut off all communication. So I was incommunicado. And when I came out of the wilderness, I homesteaded. But I basically stayed incommunicado, for many years.

When you say you went into the wilderness, you mean…

We were in the mountains, on horseback. My wife and I went together. When we left the city, we went out west, and she came with me into the mountains. We stayed for five years, hunting and gathering, living in the wilderness.

You stayed for five years? Just the two of you, out in the elements? How could you even do that?

It's not that it was easy. We gave up comfort. We'd be without food, or freezing cold, or soaking wet. In the rainy season we'd be wet for weeks at a time. I mean it was a rough life. But when I first went, it was a matter of survival. If I hadn't gone into the mountains, I'd be gone. I had to do it. And my wife was with me.

She was as wild as you!

And I'll always give her absolute credit. I could never dismiss what she did. It was beyond the norm. I couldn't have done it without her.

Your life is unreal. You go from New York City to living in the wilderness? It's hard to even imagine!

It's almost unimaginable. And I cannot tell you how or why, but I felt so comfortable, or I don't know how to put it… I don't know if I overcame my discomfort, but I felt like "this is where I am. So I better figure it out." I figured that one out. Now I gotta figure this one out.

I guess it's hard to imagine your life before that, too. I mean the intensity.

I can't really explain it, in words…Like one time, we were scouting. It was early on, so we were scouting the land. And we stopped somewhere to spend the night. Well the sheriff came and said that we were trespassing. To us that didn't mean anything, you know, we were just there. But he insisted that we had to move, we had to get out. We were being removed, so to speak.

So we start to get things together and get ready to move. And the sheriff points at our dog. He says "you can't take the dog, so I'll just have to kill him." He goes to the car and opens the trunk, and takes out a shotgun. As soon as I see the gun, I take out my pistol. I'm wearing a poncho, so the sheriff doesn't see it. I've got the pistol fixed on him. My wife is standing next to me and I tell her, "if he goes to shoot the dog, I'm gonna kill him." So she pleads with him, "why would you do that, he's just a dog, you can't kill him." And she prevailed. She knew that if I killed the sheriff, there was no way I could get away.

You just knew you had to. You knew you would.

There was no way I would allow him to kill my dog. I never even thought about it, like "should I or shouldn't I." It was just "you kill my dog, I kill you."

Then it was a good thing your wife was there! She was able to convince him not to?

She convinced him, luckily for me. And for him. Especially for him!

In a way it shows how you had freed yourself. I mean if he's about to shoot the dog, and the only way to stop him is to shoot him, then that's what you would do.

And I can't explain it. I mean, can you imagine that state of mind? But that's how we were. We were beyond…I don't know how to convey it. It almost doesn't sound real.

DAY EIGHT

Let's get back to the story: you and your wife went to the mountains, and started living in the wilderness. But how did you do it? Like how did you prepare? What season was it when you first went in?

It was probably spring. We waited out the first winter. We were trying to scout. We got horses, you know, we got pack saddles, we'd go trade. We would ride some. But we didn't totally leave civilization, at first. We stayed mostly around the communes.

So it's really remote, like big mountains right?

Up to 10,000 feet!

You were camping in a tent?

We had a tent, and we built shelters. It depended how long we were going to stay at one camp. We had the horses so we would ride, set up camp different places.

And you were able to survive by hunting and gathering? All

these things you learned just by experience?

Well you do it, or die. Like in the beginning I was not a great hunter. But our lives depended on it. It wasn't a hobby. I had to do it. So I had to get good at it. Until I got good enough, I had to just struggle along. I would go days sometimes I couldn't get any game.

Because you wouldn't give up and go get pizza or something.

And there's no place to go! Either you get the food out there, or you don't eat.

What were you hunting?

Deer and elk. Or we'd get small game like rabbit, squirrel, wild chicken, wild turkey. Like I'd be out hunting, and my wife would see small game and she would shoot it. She was a good shot.

That's really wild.

It was a wild life. Especially after the Lower East Side. But I always used to think, it's really not that different. There's a parallel, I don't know…

Somehow you deal with both environments in a similar way, I guess?

And you deal with it just as a living thing.

Also you had horses. How did you adjust to that, coming from the city?

First of all, I wasn't born in the city. I was born in the country. Second of all, even in the city I was always around horses. I worked with horses. I worked at the bridle path in Central Park, I worked at all the horse stables. One time someone from King Ranch saw me and wanted to train me as a jockey!

You could have had a whole different life! You think you could have been a jockey?

I was like 14 years old, and my mother said "no, you're not going to Kentucky."

But that's amazing how these different elements in your life are present in different moments.

That's what made it possible to live as I did. I wasn't just a city kid. I was born in the country, along the Potomac River. We had relatives on both sides, Virginia and Maryland. That was a whole world. There were reservations, that was Algonquian country. I used to stay there when I was a kid. Up until I was 10, when my mother remarried, I would go back and forth.

And I always felt grateful that in the first ten years of my life, I had a lot of interaction with non-urban life. I wasn't just a product of urban life. That really shaped me. Because I was able to experience both, I could understand both. I wasn't stuck with one or the other. I could move between environments. To tell you the truth, I don't think that I could have done what I did, if I was just a city kid. Could you imagine a city kid going to the wilderness to live? On horseback, hunting and gathering? It's almost unimaginable.

How about your wife? How did she do?

Well she did it, but it was hard for her. To be without food, or cold, or soaking wet, for weeks. I would come across her at times and she'd be crying. Life would be so hard sometimes. And no matter how hard, she took it like, "that's life." She was strong enough. But it was really hard on her.

What about the others from the family who went out west, how did they handle the shift?

Well nobody went totally into the wilderness in the way that we did. A few people tried, they followed our example and did it. But for most people there was some transition. Like there were the communes, they were part city, part country. And people from the city could fit in. And then some of them became more country. So there was this transition, or mixture.

There were a lot of communes, I guess? Because it's not only from New York but like from San Francisco and different cities, all these people were moving out to the country and making communes, right?

That was the Back to the Land movement. A lot of them went to New Mexico and Colorado, and to California. A lot also went to Vermont. And the communes were mostly New Age, counterculture, what people call "hippie." But there were some that we were closer to, that we fit in with.

Most New Age communes, you wouldn't fit in with?

No. We had a rough edge, you know, the Lower East Side was rough. So we always had this edge. We weren't hippies. And you could feel it. We looked a little like hippies, but you could feel that there was a difference. And some people were apprehensive of us.

They were suspicious, like who are these intense people from the city?

Not suspicious, but some people were uncomfortable, or they didn't understand us. Or they disagreed with our belief in self-defense, which meant violence. And they disliked us for that.

I guess someone coming from a New Age commune in New Mexico would have a hard time imagining Lower East Side life.

Exactly. And not only were we from the Lower East Side, we were on the warrior side of it. But there were also some communes with people a little bit like that.

You mean militant? Like more politicized, rather than just New Age.

Yeah, or mixed.

So after you left New York you still had contact with some people?

Mostly I was incommunicado. A lot of people thought I was dead, and I encouraged that. But some people from my family came and stayed a while. At some point most people scattered. So it was transitional somewhat.

You were in New Mexico? Or where were you, exactly?

It's a mountainous region that expands across northern New Mexico and southern Colorado. It has nothing to do with the state, the state is just a line. It's one region. And that's where we stayed. And so we would cross, like say we were in New Mexico and the Forest Service tried to find us, so we'd cross the border into Colorado. And vice versa, when Colorado got too hot, we'd cross back into New Mexico. I would send postcards to the Forest Service headquarters, like "you can stop looking, I'm in another state!" They could tell it was true by the postmark.

That's convenient, two different states.

And that was still border country then. It used to be part of Mexico. There were actually people who lived along this border that didn't really speak English. I mean it was remote, it was like a hidden area. And authority had no hold. There was no law, everybody was armed.

So it was relatively autonomous? It makes sense that you were drawn there.

Totally. There was no police. The law was enforced by people themselves. If you rustled a cow, they didn't call the police, they'd just shoot you! There was no local police, and the state police never went there. This whole area was self-governing. Like the people we joined in New Mexico in their uprising. They sensed that they were being encroached upon by an artificial law — and they rebelled.

There was an uprising? And you joined it?

Correct. They had been occupied by the National Guard. And they had written to us that they needed more people like us. You know, people with guns. So we went. There were about ten of us that went.

All of you ready to fight with guns? That's a big deal.

And we had been at that point of relocating anyway. We weren't sure how, or where, or what. Then we got this letter.

But that's a big move in terms of confrontation. Like against the National Guard, in this remote little area, that's pretty intense.

Yeah, the state police had roadblocks around this area, so you couldn't go in or out if you were known. And some of my comrades got spotted at the roadblocks. They had arms, and they were arrested.

What was happening before, would you give us the context of the uprising?

Way back, in this border region, the Spanish government gave communities what they called a land grant. It gave them the right to use the land communally, to graze their animals. So that everybody has their little plot where they live and grow food, and then they have some thousands of acres to graze their herds. It's an ideal. Grazing tribes around the world do that. There's no land grant, it's just the fact of life. It's based on use, not ownership.

So there's an immediate conflict with the American legal system. Wealthy Americans used the law to possess land, to say "this is mine, you can't graze on my land." And they got the sheriff's department to enforce it. The conflict intensified, and there was a rebellion. They raided the courthouse, there was a shootout. Then the National Guard occupied. And that was when they wrote to us.

Were you surprised to get this kind of request?

No. It was a logical request.

But did you know each other before? Or they knew of you somehow?

There was one person that knew of us. Really she knew me. There was a woman who was in SNCC, she had been involved in the South with the Freedom Rides. She was a militant. And she was part Mexican, so she got involved in the Mexican-American struggle. She joined the uprising, and she was living there amongst them. So she was the one that wrote to us. The others didn't know us.

Was it difficult to communicate? Or you had people that could translate?

No, they all spoke English. They were not deep in that part of the population that didn't speak English. They had a town, a little town way up in the mountains. Whereas it was the more rural people, the rural rancheros, that didn't interact with English speakers.

You really got to know the land, and the people and these histories. It must be beautiful there.

Yeah, it's beautiful country.

Had you been there before to that part of the country?

Not really. We went there once to take part in the great bus race. You know Ken Kesey's bus, called *Further*? And then the Hog Farm had a bus, the *Road Hog*. And then we had a bus. So we had a race. I used to argue with Ken Kesey that we won, but actually I have no idea. I was so stoned I didn't even know what was going on, you know, I couldn't tell you who won for real. But I used to always tease him, "hey we won that race!"

Those were very different conditions, your first and second time to New Mexico. Wow.

You know sometimes, when I hear myself, I almost can't believe it. Like when I talk about the things we did, how different they were, how extreme on so many different levels, from the counterculture, to the militancy, to the art — I'm almost like "wow, did we do all that?" It almost sounds like a fantasy.

To me too, it sounds like a dream. I'm still amazed by this story of the uprising. As it turned out, when you left the city it wasn't a retreat from armed struggle. It was an escalation!

And that was also a transitional moment. I was ready to die in the struggle. But at the same time, I had this sense that there was something missing. Something was needed, beyond art and politics. I was seeking something other than what was available to me in the city.

I could never quite formulate it. Not even what the question would be. I just sensed there was something missing. So when I felt that it was time to leave New York, or when I more or less had to leave, it was not only the impetus to leave, but I thought, "this is my chance to see what this other thing is." I didn't have a clear idea of what it was. But I knew that it was necessary.

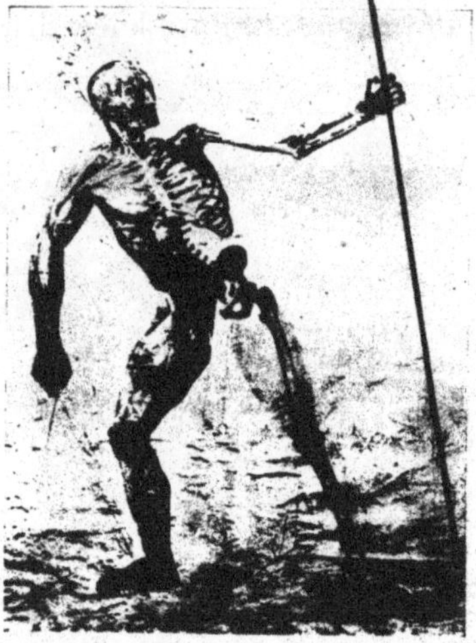

Revolution in dreams
Revolution in books
Revolution in cars
Revolution in advertising

but everywhere repression.

repressed living as the
expression of everyday life

And your biggest enemy is your ASS.

pick it up
let it move
Make it happen

is anything else in nature straight = NO =
where the fuck did it come from?
From your fucking heads.

Can you sleep with Che under dorm regulations?
Will Aretha Franklin sing the 6th International?
Can you MOVE!

Street music:
Tactical Pig Symphony vs. the Invisible Street Band / banned / ban
BAMN
By Any Means Necessary

And despite everything the man can do--we will survive, we will grow,
and dig it--we will win!
Make It Happen.

The Bossman (No-Balls/man) sees the threat of the Street whore luring "his" young from the programmed possibility of their existence into the only real possibility of existence -- luring the worker's sons from factory smoke to the smoke of the burning factories--And now "living" is possible for everyone.

"Poor Dad, too bad, Momma hung you in the closet and I'm feelin'
so sad."
So pick his pockets
Take his watch
Steal his gold teeth----

And Support you local Revolution -- MAKE IT HAPPEN

up against the wall/motherfuckers (IWWC)

DAY NINE

Ben, it's exciting today. We've been looking forward to this part of the story. You lived in the wilderness for five years. What was it like? What was the daily routine? Like in the morning you woke up, then what did you eat for breakfast?

Our main diet was dry meat. My wife would prepare it different ways, breakfast, lunch and dinner. But that was the main ingredient. Then sometimes we would have some grain, there was a wild grain you could harvest. On occasion we would trade with country stores that were up high, and we'd get oatmeal or something and mix it with meat. And we'd get small game like squirrel or rabbit. So it would vary, depending on what we had. Like my wife would find certain vegetables and that would be the dinner, she'd make soups or other things. Lunch we basically just had meat ground up in a tortilla, my wife would make tortillas. She did all the cooking. She was really good at it.

You would butcher the animals yourself?

My wife did all of that. I would hunt and she would butcher it, then cut it into strips and dry it.

She did all the butchering? That's hard core.

See I was out hunting all day, and she was at camp. So she did the butchering and cooking, she got firewood, she would go and forage. We had a balance. I'd be out hunting ten hours a day, and she used that time in camp.

You went hunting on horseback, or on foot?

Mainly on foot. You would use the horse maybe to go a certain distance. But the horse scares off the animals.

What did you forage? I guess you ate a lot of mushrooms.

Totally, mushrooms were a main part of our diet. For instance a puffball: it's the size of a basketball. If you cut it up it's four or five meals! There are tons of wild vegetables. You just have to know what they are.

One time, my wife found some mushrooms. She cooked them and we had them for breakfast. But something didn't feel right. I told her "you know, that mushroom was really greasy." Well she'd put no grease in it, she just cooked it in a frying pan. She said "why don't you look it up?" We had some pamphlets about different plant species that we carried with us. So she said "why don't you check, see if you could find that mushroom." I looked, and I found it. I said "here it is, I found it." She said "well, read it to me." "Alright," I said.

"This mushroom is extremely deadly."

I looked at my wife and she was waiting like, what else does it say? Then I read:

"The toxins in this mushroom can cause you to break into uncontrollable laughter."

As I was reading this, I started laughing. I couldn't stop. Then my wife broke out laughing. I said "oh shit, we're in trouble." We passed out. We went unconscious for at least a day, maybe two days. We were *out*.

Then when you woke up that must have been pretty intense, realizing that you'd almost died.

Yeah, if I were normal. But I just got up and said, "I better go hunting! We need something to eat!"

It really is hard to imagine that life. Like for someone who's never spent more than a day or two outside – let alone what you all did.

Twenty four hours a day. For five years!

The world would change! You would become a different person.

I did. I came out after five years no longer the same person. I was not a Lower East Side person anymore. I changed.

So these years were really important for you, for your transformation.

Crucial. Who I am, would not be without that experience. I went into the wilderness with nothing. No money, no credit cards, no identity. I gave it all up. I wanted to see what I really needed. What do we need to live? And that's what led me eventually towards animism.

Also you gradually got close to Native American community.

Correct. And I got involved with this animistic, ceremonial world.

I imagine the experience of being in the wilderness was important to get to know those people.

I'm sure it played a part. It wasn't the only part. But it was important, there's no question. Like when we came out of the wilderness, the first place we came out there was a reservation. We were on horseback, and they said "well you could camp on our land by our house." So we pitched our tent by their house. It was like they felt immediate kinship to us. I'm sure the way we were living helped.

What about the others that went out west with you from the city? You talked about the idea of building alternative worlds, but that's a little different from your vision of trying to find out what is really needed.

That goes back to what I call the Pancho Villa syndrome. I wanted to see what was necessary to live. And how to live in the world, so to speak. Some of the others felt like the revolution had failed, and they no longer cared about changing the world. So they became bandits. It happens everywhere in the world where revolution doesn't succeed. A lot of revolutionaries turn to banditry. Because the ingredients are there: they're armed and they're ready to die.

Also they believe in counter-power. They're against the ruling order.

So they remained anti-establishment, and anti-centralization. But they became self-absorbed. They were no longer fighting a revolution. Now it was just for benefit, and to survive.

They became bandits meaning like, armed robbery and such?

Yeah, they got fixated with that…I'll show you an example. There was a railroad that still ran through the mountains, like a narrow gauge. Tourists would take it. Well, they got to a point where they were gonna stop the train and rob it! You know like in movies where the bandits come out on horseback and hold up the train. They had this fantasy that they were gonna do that.

Wait, seriously? Like the image from the Wild West!

Yeah. They were gonna do it! They got together in the mountains and they were gonna ride down and rob the train. But we found out about it and we went to them, we caught them at night when they were in bed. We put guns to their heads and said "if you do it, we're gonna come back and kill you."

You wanted to stop them?

Because that would destroy our way of life. Nobody could live in the mountains after that! They would be occupied by federal forces. And they would find everybody that was living on horseback.

And yet they wanted to act out this image from the Wild West.

Yeah well, they were romantics. The imagery is exciting, like WOW, all of a sudden these guys come down on horseback and rob the train! And you can't blame them for the thought, it *is* an exciting thought. But the reality was like, wait a minute. We're not doing that.

They were only involved in the imagery, and their self-aggrandizement. They got fixated on their own mythology. They weren't thinking about what would happen to the rest of us in the mountains.

They were trying to do guerrilla warfare?

No, they were trying to do guerrilla crime. The revolution was over, in their minds. They were doing it as criminals. You know, it's exciting! You can't explain it to anybody…To be armed and ready to die and just do whatever you want. It's like a drug.

And you all had such powerful experiences, right? I mean you did have that power, in the Lower East Side.

It was for a purpose though.

For revolution.

And to help people that needed help. But they were doing it to help themselves.

So the family that went with you from New York, they became like a bandit gang out west?

Or different groups would form, with new recruits.

When you say new recruits, that's not necessarily political people I guess?

No. They were mercenaries. They were already bandits. And they figured they'd get together and become bandit gangs.

Can I ask, in the city you also carried guns: that was more for protection, like against the police?

The police, or whatever.

Because you told us also that you did security for the Black Panthers. You were sort of armed guards, helping other radicals with your guns?

On that one occasion. Generally speaking, it was for self-defense. There were also predators, you know, the city was tough. The Lower East Side was an extreme ghetto. And there were people preying on these young runaways, and out to exploit them or steal from them or attack them — I mean it was tough.

I wonder if your idea of self-defense is part of your idea of freedom? Or like autonomy, today a lot of people use that

word. In your time, in the '60s, maybe self-defense was very important for autonomy.

Well if you can't defend yourself, then you're a victim. If people can't protect themselves, how can they be free? I mean, do you know how many young people were assaulted, sexually, on these streets? We used to walk around and protect them. We had patrols at night looking out for them, sending them to our crash pads.

So that's the thing, when you say "self-defense" it's not just you all.

No, self-defense meaning defense of people. As in, we need to do it for ourselves. To protect our own people. We don't need police.

It was really a symbiotic relationship with those kids.

You have no idea how wild it was. There was nothing like it. One time, some people with malicious intent had kidnapped some young people and had them in an apartment, and some people came running and told us, they got these kids in this room. We went and we broke the door down, we were armed, and we freed the kids.

Wasn't it scary? To fight against people like that?

Listen, it's no more scary to fight against some predator than it is to fight against the US government. They'll both kill you. We didn't differentiate. If they were the enemy of what we were trying to do, it didn't matter if it was governmental or criminal.

Even amongst ourselves, like when those guys were gonna rob the train. We went to them and threatened them, we said "if you do it, we're gonna kill you. We'll go to war." So we were acting like our own defense. You know, we're not law enforcement, but to us this was gonna bring so much heat on the mountains, it would interfere with our living there. It would be the end of the culture that we were trying to build.

And you had to use force, you couldn't just say "hey stop doing this." You had to threaten them.

You couldn't just say "well we're against it." I mean we didn't have a meeting and take a vote. That's what people can't understand. It's not that we *had* the right; we *made* the right. Put guns to their heads and say "next time, we'll kill you."

Wow, it really was the Wild West. I can't believe this whole bandit world.

Almost nobody knows what that world was like.

It's a world I've never imagined before. So it was you all from the city, and then some people local to the area, just came together and started living this bandit kind of life?

And from different places, like from the West Coast, people gravitated to the mountains. And they heard about it, "wow these guys are living on horseback!" And it just spread. At some point there were a couple hundred of us!

Really? The authorities didn't stop you?

They would if they could find you. That's why we tried to stop people from doing outrageous things that would bring heat on the mountains. But you know, this was fifty years ago, everything was different. Like there was no GPS, they couldn't scan the land. So not only could they not find you, but they couldn't even tell you were there. That's not the case today.

Everyone was living in the wilderness, like hunting and camping?

Yeah or some had little cabins, or ranch houses, or they would stay in abandoned houses. Most were transient. It was just a general group of renegades living in the mountains. We didn't all stay together. There were different bands of people. But we would assemble occasionally.

Like one time, some of them had a shootout with the state police. And one guy got shot, he was wounded, so he couldn't get away. He collapsed and the state troopers found him. They took him and put him in a prison hospital. And he escaped, eventually he got back into the mountains. Then not long after that, he got into some conflict, and he got killed. That happened sometimes, you know, people would fight amongst themselves. So people were often getting killed.

Anyway, this guy had made it clear that he wanted to be cremated. So word got out to all the mountain people. We picked a spot and stacked logs to make a pyre, and put his body on top and then lit it. Well, I guess the Forest Service saw the fire. Suddenly this truck pulls up, and this guy jumps out and starts yelling, "put it out! Put out that fire!" I look at him and say, "*you* put it out." Then he looks around and sees there's like two hundred of us, everybody's looking at him. And we're armed, we're like wild, mountain people. You could see this was not a normal crowd. The guy was like, "uh-oh." He jumped back in the truck and they left!

That's amazing. And totally impossible today.

Totally. There were no cell phones then, and we were way in the mountains. They had to go down themselves to get reinforcement. By the time they got back everybody was gone.

The technology was different, and the land itself was part of it. The mountains allowed for it, in a way.

And throughout this whole region, authority didn't exist. It was so remote. I mean I came across people that didn't really speak English, like the Mexican population, or mixed Mexican and Native American. There were Apaches around there, a lot of them didn't move when the government moved the Apaches. A lot of them went and hid. Some were married to Mexicans and refused to move. So there were already people living out there that were like a mountain people. They'd been out there living normal lives. Then this new group would just fit in. They could get lost, so to speak.

They blended together.

Well, they blended together, and they also helped each other in a sense.

Did any of the people who were already out there get wrapped up in it?

Some did. But most didn't.

The situation today must be so different. For either kind of group of people, it must be much more difficult now to sustain that kind of autonomy.

Oh, it's impossible now. This is fifty years ago we're talking about! Now most want to be American. You heard of Billy the Kid? His great-grandson lived out there, and he didn't even speak English hardly. He was mostly Mexican. His last name was Bonney, which was a Scottish name that Billy the Kid used. I knew him, I used to go visit him. He lived in San Geronimo, New Mexico. I used to ride out there on horseback and stop and visit him.

Wait, really? This time you must be kidding!

See that's what I mean: this is a dying world we're talking about.

Something else replaces it, I'm not saying it's over. But what that was that we're talking about is not ever going to happen again.

So to build autonomy we have to discover something in the present.

That's the job of the people who are in the present. I'm already past it. I mean, not totally. I have a foot still in it, but…

I think you've got more than a foot! But it's interesting, this bandit phenomenon. There's some paradox. To have this power and freedom, but then it self-destructs. It implodes, the group can't cohere.

That's the Pancho Villa syndrome. A lot of revolutionaries become bandits. Pancho Villa is a classic case, that's why I call it Pancho Villa syndrome. But it happened all over the world. Like Mahkno in the Ukraine, they became bandits. It happened in Spain, it happened in Brazil — it was heavy in Brazil. It happened everywhere.

What about you? Weren't you drawn down the Pancho Villa path?

I avoided it by searching out a deeper need. The spiritual need. And eventually that led to animism, and helped me to see how my efforts could still help to change the world for the better. I found a way to continue the struggle on another level. A lot of the others forgot about all of that. You know the revolution didn't happen, so let's just…

When they sensed that the revolution failed, it's like they were depressed, they became nihilistic?

Well, no. But they came to a place where they realized that what they had been doing was no longer plausible. It's hard to put it in words. You'd have to experience it. But if you're a revolutionary, and you are armed and you are ready to die, what do you do when there's no revolution? Become a dentist? I mean what do you do? So you remain armed, you remain ready to die. But you have to survive.

A lot of them didn't survive it. A lot of them got killed. They got killed in fights with state police, they killed each other in arguments. At least ten of them died in that struggle. More than in the street struggle.

It must have been hard for you being one of the ones to make it out. You must have been so worried.

Yeah, well, it was hard. My kid brother got killed. He became a bandit, and he got killed by other bandits. He got shot.

None of the others followed, or went with you?

I often thought about it, at the time. About my kid brother especially. I could see that he was headed for destruction. And I talked to him, I told him about the other path that I was on. I tried to see if I could get him to go with me. But I couldn't get it through to him, at first. It didn't happen fast enough I guess.

I wonder what the difference was between you and the others. Maybe if they had shared your sense of searching...

I would be reluctant to say. You can't tell. But no one from that world entered the world I was entering.

DAY TEN

Ben, I was thinking about the first time we met.

I remember, it was in Brooklyn.

At the Wyckoff space. We were at the same party.

That was early on, when I had just reemerged.

At first I didn't know who you were. But you were very sweet and friendly, and we had a nice talk. Then later I realized "oh that was Ben Morea!" And I was shocked. My image of you, I thought Ben Morea was kind of scary, like a scary biker man.

That's why I never look in the mirror. I'm scary!

You know, I found some pictures from when you were younger. I could only find a few. But you really did look scary.

Yeah, I used to be more intense.

Still I believe you must have been very kind. Like towards the kids, you must have been warm and open.

I was. But I was an intense person.

Will you tell us about your decision to come back to the city? Why did you resurface, after so many years away?

Well, I don't know how, but someone found out how to reach me. And she called and asked me to come to the city to speak. I told her "absolutely not. I haven't been there for forty years. I'm on some other trajectory, I'm involved with other energies. And the last thing I want to do is get back into the political ideological crowd." So I told her "no," I apologized and hung up.

But I kept thinking about it. I first entered the world of resistance because I felt that things have to change, I decided I had to do something. Well, the world in the '60s was not as bad off as it is now. It's actually worse now. So I felt bad saying "no I won't come back." And so I called her, I said "I'll try it. But don't do a lot of advertising. If you keep it low key, I'll try it and see if I fit, see what kind of questions people ask, how do I respond." So they had a small gathering at a space called 16 Beaver. That was the first time I spoke publicly since the '60s.

At first it was a little difficult for me. But I became comfortable with it, and I felt some sense of accomplishment. And then somebody mentioned there's another place we want you to speak. I said "okay I'll try it." And that was bigger, like a hundred people. Then somebody approached me and said they wanted to have a big assembly at the New School. And that was like 500 people. At that point I felt comfortable enough. So that was how it happened. It just kept growing.

That was also the time of Occupy right? Like 2011?

The New School was around Occupy. The earlier ones were before. You know, I'm no good with dates. But I felt like it was something that I had to engage myself in. I felt like, I'd spent forty years away, and things have gotten worse, if anything. And if I really wanted to see a change, I should contribute.

How would you describe how the world got worse?

It just feels like we've reached a point of larger tragedy. You know, with the environment, and now the pandemic, it's like the whole thing is coming unglued. In the '60s we had a big struggle, but it was pretty clear what it was — you know, the struggle. But now it seems larger. The whole Earth is threatened with extinction. Everything is exacerbated.

You said you left the political ideological crowd behind when you left the city. How did you find the political milieu, when you came back?

In the '60s there were a lot of Trotskyists, Maoists, you know, different Marxists. And I had to spend time dealing with them. When I came back, it seemed there was a more open community, and a lot were less ideological. So it was more of an open base, less controlled. It felt like more fertile ground. I didn't want to get into those internecine battles.

What kinds of questions were people asking? Did you feel that you could respond, you were able to connect with people?

In the beginning I was really nervous if there would be a focus on where I went and what I did those forty years I was away. I didn't want to talk about that. But if people were more interested in what happened in the '60s, and how it pertains to today, that was a conversation that I felt more comfortable with. So I was anxious to see what the orientation would be. I found that most people wanted to talk about the '60s. Or they wanted to talk about art. Or about Valerie Solanas, some groups mainly asked about her. Every place I spoke, the questions were different. And there were less questions like "where did you go, what did you do?" So I felt more comfortable with dialogue.

And slowly I began to find a way to articulate what I did, and what I learned during those forty years, that would not pose a threat to where I went. I formulated a conversation around general terms. Like animism. Where I came from, the people were animists. But I didn't want to identify those people. They had made room for me in their world. In no way would I expose it. But animism as an understanding, I saw could be introduced.

So now I'm comfortable proselytizing and expanding the concepts of animism, as a necessity. I personally believe that we cannot address the problems of the world without animism. Period. Capitalism is doomed. Religious ideology and theology are doomed. The humanist, materialist concept is over. But what replaces it? You have to have an understanding that transcends them. And to me, animism is what is necessary. To understand that we are part of something greater. We are not in control.

The humanist conception perceives the human as a pinnacle, above other forms of creation. And that's a mistake. We're no better. We have a different consciousness. But it's not like other life forms are insignificant. They are as significant as us. And we have to understand how to interact with it. We're just part of this larger reality. Until we understand that, we'll never get along with it.

In the city everything is imported, commercial, provided. It seems like where you went, you did something different. You had to find food, you were exposed to the weather. And that also changed your perception of everything.

Totally. And that's what I did, it was not an ideological search. It was a search for an alternative. It wasn't a search for another ideology. It was a search for another *way of life*.

You said that you changed a lot, from this experience.

To be honest, this might sound extreme — if I hadn't changed, I'd be dead. This way of life allowed me to change. If you're stuck with an urban consciousness, you can't survive it.

Will you say more about how?

You have to begin to understand that nature is in control. You're in its domain. It's not in your domain. You're in its domain, and you have to find a way to live with it. To be part of it. If you resist it, or antagonize it, you're done!

That's the beginning of animist understanding: we have to find a way to fit into nature. Nature doesn't have to fit us. That's what the Western, capitalist mind thinks, that nature is there for us to use. That's how some people have destroyed the environment. They think of it only as a resource that they can use to make money, with no consciousness of what harm it might do. So they extract things from the Earth that they should have left alone. They do things with animals that they should not have done. That's why we have pandemics! Their actions caused the pandemic. And if they don't change, there will be future pandemics. The next one will be worse. Same with the storms, hurricanes, tsunamis, wildfires, drought, all of that. They're only going to get worse.

I don't know how to put it exactly, to make it clearer. But there's a connection between what you do, and how nature responds.

That's what you experienced directly when you were living in the wilderness. You had to learn how to interact.

Not only to learn, but you have to accept your role as a subservient part of a greater whole. You're no longer in charge. See, that's why the overuse of science is dangerous. It's not that I'm against science. But the capitalist world thinks it can correct the problem through science. You can't correct the problem through science. Science can maybe help to explain to you the problem. But you can only correct the problem by understanding nature, and changing your relation to it.

I like that way of thinking, to say that animism is a way for us to understand nature. That's usually how we think about science. But you're saying that actually, as an understanding of nature, animism is more powerful than science.

And animism is a way of understanding that the universe is alive. It's a living thing. It's one. You are part of that one. You are not in charge of it. You are only part of it. And if you understand that you are part of it, then your need is not to control other parts. Your need is to coexist, and be part of the whole process.

I mean think about it: *the universe.* Do you know how many stars, how many galaxies there are? We're talking billions, they can't even count them! And these idiots running around thinking that we are the center — of what? The Earth is not even a speck in terms of the universe.

For you, the sense of being part of it involves the sense of being small?

Being infinitesimal.

Being part means being infinitesimal?

Because the whole is so great that if you're part of it, you're infinitesimal. And you have no choice. It's not up to you to decide.

Also there's infinity in the smallness. So both ways, it's beyond us.

Right. Like in Tantric philosophy there's a saying: "if it exists here, it exists everywhere." I always remember that saying because it's so true. Whatever entity exists in the universe, it's all made up of the same elements, like hydrogen or oxygen or whatever. So what exists in the universe, exists in us. There's a whole universe in each of us. You're a walking universe! So we're both: we are a universe, but we are also part of the universe.

So it's an insignificance, but it's a connection. But it's hard to sense that connection maybe? Or I feel like people are aware and afraid of their insignificance, but not so much their connection.

Actually I would say most Western people, not all people, but in Western culture they don't think that they are part of something greater, they think that they *are* something greater. That's the mistake. They feel like "wow we're reaching this"...They're not reaching anything! The further you reach the further you get away from what's real. Like they got to the atom bomb, and they think that's a high point. They're getting closer to extinction by the day!

And they say that's progress for humanity.

They think it's a high point that humans have been able to understand the force of an atom. It was always there in nature, and so to understand it is one thing. But to recreate it is going to bring you to doom.

And the audacity — like America has hydrogen bombs. And they want to keep other countries from having nuclear bombs. Like they're trying to keep Iran from having nuclear bombs. Meanwhile Israel has nuclear bombs. Well, if Israel could have them, and the US could have them, anybody could have them. I mean that's logical. The US is not special.

They think they rule the world. And the war is always with non-Westerns.

They *think*. But what they forget is that nature rules the world. Nature doesn't need an atom bomb. It *is* an atom bomb!

Right, the sun is the atom bomb.

And if you get to a point where you're in the way, and nature doesn't want you there, you're gone! That's what's happening now. Nature's saying "that's enough. You messed up enough."

So we have to recognize, people have to recognize that they're only part of it. They're not in control. The human is not the pinnacle of creation. The human is part of this creation — and only a part. Until we understand that, we'll never get it right.

But to change the concepts of the human mind — a revolution is easy compared to changing the way people think. That's overwhelming! That's going to take a lot of work, and a long time.

For you it was a long process of changing your thinking, changing your way of living...How do you think about it?

I actually put in words in my mind: I wanted to go back to ground zero and see what I really needed. I went into the wilderness with nothing. I gave it all up! I gave it up to see what is really needed. What do we need to live? And that's what led me towards animism: understanding that I am part of this larger reality.

That was a decision you came to, it was like an intuition you had when you left New York?

Yeah, I had that thought before I left. But I didn't know how to implement it. Like I kept sensing that art and politics were important. But they weren't enough. There's something missing, what is it?

I had to give up all material comfort to find out, what do we need. And it was a spiritual awakening. It was an animistic understanding that I could not have found if I had stayed in the city.

DAY ELEVEN

We are waiting for your revelation today. Because we always come here thinking "we're going to ask Ben this or that." And you always introduce something great and totally unexpected. A new subject opens up every time. So we don't have to ask you anything!

Actually, there is something I was thinking about. Use the metaphor of a car, say you have a car and different parts start to break down. The starter goes out, then the transmission goes out, then the radiator. You wouldn't say "well it's a starter problem," or "it's a faulty transmission." You would begin to realize that the whole car is just old — or not even just old, but it reached the point where it's no longer viable.

But people don't look at culture that way. There's global warming, there's nuclear disaster, now there's the pandemic: nobody says they're all part of one problem. Instead they treat each issue separately. They want to solve the pandemic, so they make a vaccine. They want to solve global warming, so they cut greenhouse gasses. They don't recognize that the culture itself is malfunctioning, and that's the source of all these breakdowns. It's really one problem, in a sense. And you'll never solve the real issue if you treat them each separately. The only way to solve it is to recreate the whole cultural reality. The whole thing. To recognize something is wrong with this way of life. This culture, or whatever term you want to use. Something is wrong.

And that's not really addressed by the Left, as far as I can see. Do you think?

Maybe people try to think of the totality, but some just focus on the economy, or the environment, or discrimination. But not the intricate relationship between these powers.

I was thinking about it, in other words I think that everybody has to confront it in their realm. So people who are involved in political struggle, that's where they're going to confront the problem. But at the same time, you have to consider it in its entirety. You can't say it's only a political problem.

Say a person who's a school teacher, they have to deal with it in the classroom. That's where they are every day. So they have to find a way to deal with it, to bring some understanding to their students. Or a person who's an artist, they have to deal with it in their art. Whatever world you're involved in, that's where you're going to deal with it. But even though that's where your main energy is focused, you have to address it as part of the larger problem.

To recreate the whole cultural reality, you said? That's a major reframing.

And that's the only way…It may not be solved in our time. It may not be solved for generations to come. But we have to at least lay the groundwork so that it can be solved.

See that's why, to me, the political struggle alone is not enough. It's not just politics and the economy: you have to deal with the universe! In other words, the universe is the reality. And we have to figure out how to fit in it.

Cosmic politics! That may be something only you can say, Ben, to frame the struggle in terms of the universe.

Maybe I'm the only person foolish enough.

But in a sense you are doing it, in your life. Like living in the wilderness, you established a political relationship with nature, right? Mountains, stars, trees...

Right.

Bears, deer, mushrooms...You told us about getting sick from mushrooms.

I almost died. Twice!

Did you see some spirit? Like the spirit of a coyote, or a bear, or something?

No. I seen the void.

The void...

To be honest with you, I don't have any recollection of that. I was completely unconscious. You know the word "psychotropic?" Where plants induce visions and consciousness. It wasn't a psychotropic event.

Also you were hunting, so you had to learn how to track the animals and follow their movements. And you learned how to butcher and use different parts, like dry some part, or salt it. Did you ever eat raw meat?

Well, I don't want to freak anybody out. But my habit, the minute I killed a deer, was to eat the heart raw, while it's still pumping. Not the whole heart, you know they're pretty big. But part of it.

Did it taste good?

I wouldn't use the term "good" or "bad." It's a way of joining with the animal, on some other level. I don't know what word to use, words are so limited. But it's a way of recognizing its life force. It's not just meat, like "I got food so I'm gonna eat it." Instead you're communing with it. Rather than treat it as an object, as a dead animal, you treat it as life. It was living, breathing, still pumping…And eating the beating heart was a way of connecting with the life I received.

One time, you won't believe this, but one time I shot a deer in the heart. And it kept running. It ran maybe a thousand yards. And when I found it and gut it, I saw that the heart was split in two pieces. That's how powerful the will to live is. The deer had run that distance with its heart split in two.

You felt awe?

Absolutely. It's a spiritual thing. To realize that the effort to live, the force of life is so strong that it could run with its heart split. It's not just the deer, it's this life force. It's the same with all life. Even viruses, like now with the pandemic — they're not going to just give up now that there's a vaccine. No, there's a vaccine and they're gonna fight it, they're gonna mutate and survive. Because it's a living thing! And the more prevalent the vaccine becomes, the more mutations there will be.

It's like antibiotics. Antibiotics were beneficial to some degree. They found something, it could help people. Then they overused it so much that it lost its efficacy. Now there are superbugs that developed to overcome the antibiotics. That's how strong this life force is. It overcame the antibiotic.

That reminds me of these microorganisms, you know, there's microplastics everywhere. And there are organisms that are adapting to use the plastics. Some life forms are already evolving.

That's what this culture doesn't understand, that all these things are alive. And they'll do whatever they can to stay alive. They'll mutate and pass it on, so the next generation survives.

When you were hunting and you started to eat the heart, that was a kind of intuition?

It was almost instinctual. All of a sudden I realized I could connect to it. It wasn't like I thought about it in advance and decided to do it. I could just feel it.

And you would use most of the body parts, not just the meat but the heart and different organs?

All of it. Or I tried to. That's how Indigenous people are. If you're going to take the life of an animal, you should use as much as of it as possible. First of all, I would pray before I took a life. Before I went hunting, I would pray and ask permission, and say thank you. I would express gratitude for that life that I was allowed to share. I wouldn't just take it for granted.

But how did you learn how to do it, technically? You learned from others, or you had to just experiment, like how do we use this part or that part?

It's a combination. But the first thing is the recognition that if you're going to take a life, you should make use of it as much as possible. This life is so precious that if you take it, you can't waste it. You can't throw it away like it's nothing. Indigenous people knew how to use everything, even the hooves. They had a culture built on that. Being new to it, I didn't. So I'm sure that I was not as complete as they were. But I tried.

I imagine you learned a lot about plants too, like medicinal plants and such?

I did. I learned so much that I used to write a weekly article for a newspaper. For instance, you know about vitamin C, how important it is. Well the needles of a pine tree have more vitamin C than oranges. So if you live in the mountains, you don't have oranges but you've got pine trees all around. You can just take a branch off a tree.

And chew it?

Make a tea. Then there's certain plants you drink the tea from and they're blood purifiers. Like yarrow, it grows everywhere. So we would pick yarrow and make tea with it.

That's another understanding that Western culture lost: everything you put in your body is a medicine. For some Native Americans, "medicine" is the most used word. Everything is a medicine. Things you do in life are a medicine. Things you consume, food is medicine. Even earlier Western cultures understood that, how foods help the body. We're losing that more and more. Now you get a vitamin pill.

When you say that things you do in life are a medicine, what do you mean?

It's how you live. How you move. Like some older Native people have a way in their everyday life where they never turn around, they try to flow one way. I don't know how to put it into words, language is a problem…I'll show you. Say I stand up, and I start to walk over here. Then something happens, the phone rings. So I'm going to come back to answer it. I won't turn myself around. I'll just change direction and go this way, instead of turning. And come back.

You're always facing ahead, is that the idea?

Generally speaking, people in this culture are constantly turning themselves around. But some people in Native American cultures have a different consciousness of space and movement. Like when I enter a room, I know which way I came in, and I try to not turn. And that's a medicine!

That's beautiful.

But how do you tell that to people? Like how do you tell a Marxist, "don't turn around." They'll look at you like, "what? We're talking about workers, you know, labor issues. Who cares about turning around!"

Because also it's mainly unspoken, I guess. You could just notice people doing it.

Well it's unspoken but it's not unspoken. They pass it on to their children. And certain people are really strict about it. But everybody's conscious of it. In the ceremonial life, you're supposed to follow it. That's where it's absolutely imperative. Then you could go to the next level and try in your daily life. There are some people who try to carry that, continue throughout their whole life. Like myself, I try never to turn around. So that means I'm conscious of where I am, all the time.

It's about being aware of the space around you. You have to keep in mind what's behind you.

And you remember how you came in the room. You're conscious of your movement and where you are on the planet every second.

You learned that from the Native community you were with?

Well I observed, I understood it. I don't know if anybody ever said to me "don't turn." But I understood, like for instance, there are certain ceremonial people you cannot walk behind. They come into a room and they sit in the corner, or they sit with their back to the wall. So I could see that, and I began to realize that there's certain people you cannot walk behind. It's not spoken, but observed.

It's embodied, more than just verbal.

And that, to me, is the full sense of consciousness. That you are conscious of every step you make in your life. That's why I can't relate to most political people. I mean we're talking about consciousness, life — we're talking about the universe! The stars move a certain way. You never see a star go a different way! Every star goes one way. So you have to observe the universe. But you can't tell that to political people.

Because their conceptual reality is so different. It's hyper-focused on certain problems. But it's also abstracted.

And then simplicity is gone. For instance, you have a culture filled with addiction. Have you ever heard anybody say well, when the child was born, when it was growing up, you kept feeding it sugar. You gave them cereal full of sugar every day. You made them into an addict! Because then, they had to have sugar. They had to have a stimulant. And they became addicted to other stimulants. But you started them, at birth. I mean, you ever try to tell people that? They'll look at you like, "what are you talking about? Who cares about giving kids sugar?" But that's what's important! In reality, how you get your children started on addiction with sugar, is actually important. It's a simple thing, but it's consequential.

It's violent actually. It's like poison.

It's toxic! Try to tell them that. They give it to themselves. See, you can't talk to people about this stuff.

People do it every day without thinking about it. But it really is upside down, to take toxin instead of medicine.

Right. So if you think of everything as medicine: how you move, how you think, everything that affects your stability, your environment — it can expand to include everything. It's all medicine. And certain animals have medicine. To some Indigenous, what they call Native American people, like to some Plains tribes, the buffalo was not just another animal. The buffalo gave them their whole life. So to them, the buffalo has a medicine. It's not a food. It has a medicine — it's giving you life.

The idea of taste must be very different from people in the city eating chocolate or potato chips. When you eat deer heart you're not like "oh this is great, it's so tasty."

It doesn't have to be pleasing in terms of taste. It has to be satisfying on another level. But you know, I'll be honest with you, I've never talked to anybody about these things. Because how do you talk to people about what they consider to be so unimportant, or uninteresting?

Maybe the problem is the context, like you said why can political people deal with politics, but not the universe? Maybe we don't have the language, or not just language but we lack the social context for sharing these things.

Or we have no sense of how vital and important it really is.

I think that's true. The sense itself is distorted, you know, I think about taste, or about "nutrients" that I have to consume, rather than medicine. But it's really impressive, this practice of not turning around. The idea that every second, you could live in this conscious way. For most people I think awareness is channeled.

This culture has lost its senses. Nobody in this culture has the sense that the universe is here. You are in the universe right here. It's not out there waiting for a rocket ship. It's here! You are in the universe! Wake up! The universe surrounds you. How do you tell people that? I couldn't tell anybody but you guys, because somehow we got close. But you know, people would look at you like "oh man they should lock this guy up."

One last question: how about your relationship with minerals? Like you had relations with plants and animals, but how about mountains, rocks, all these things?

I don't know how to put it in words. But to me, everything is living. Rocks are living. I mean everything is living! They may even have consciousness — I don't know the words. But Indigenous peoples understood certain rocks are living. Say Ayers Rock, in Australia. That was spiritually key to Aboriginal life. Have you seen it? It's that huge rock that comes out of the ground, part of it is underground. To Aboriginal people this was spiritual, I mean it's a living thing. Well that's how I think, that everything is alive.

You wouldn't make a distinction between life and non-life.

You could make a nominal distinction. But it's not a real distinction. You could recognize that's a rock: that's a nominal distinction. But you can't say it's not alive.

There are things that don't move on their own. That doesn't make them lesser. They're inanimate, they're not moving. But they're equally important. In some way, they're more important. They're key to spiritual health. Like the planet: the planet is alive! And we are part of that life.

In Japan, mountains and rocks are worshiped.

That's the same thing. It's inanimate, it doesn't move. But it is alive. It's a medicine. And the correct way is to venerate it. It's not unimportant, like "oh it's just a rock." That's what's wrong with Western culture: it doesn't understand that.

So here you have Ayers Rock, listen to this. To Aboriginal people it's a sacred rock. Well the Australian colonizer put spikes in the rock so that people could climb it easier, like for tourists. In the sacred rock! And around the bottom they have tables and umbrellas so they can sit and drink and be around the rock.

That's disgusting.

Not only that, but do you know that in 40,000 years, Aboriginal people used a certain amount of water. That same amount of water is what the Australian colonizer now uses in one year. 40,000 years! And Aboriginal people are saying, these are reservoirs underground: what's going to happen when they're drained? We didn't overuse them. We used them sparingly. Because once they're gone, we're gone!

That's the difference in thinking between the colonizer and the Aboriginal, who the colonizer called savage. The whole thing is backwards.

It's amazing to understand the connection, to see yourself as part of a people that lives for thousands of years.

That was the consciousness of Indigenous people everywhere. But to the colonizer, you know how low the Aboriginal is thought of, almost like they're an animal. They're not even human, I mean the way the colonizer thought.

Listen to this, this will blow your mind. There's water underground, in Australia. That's where the water is. In the outback, there's no surface water. It's all underground. So in order to live out there, you have to know where to find the water. And Aboriginal people found a way, over 40,000 years they figured out: say I'm gonna go into the outback, which is thousands of miles of dryness, no water. As I start walking from here, I start singing a song. They developed these songs so that when you reach a certain point in the song, you reach a place where there's water underground. They figured out how to track the water using song. They passed the songs on to their descendants. Could you imagine that intelligence?

It's beautiful. That's art! And it's a use of language that's actually helpful.

It's everything! It's everything you could want. And almost nobody knows about it. I mean some people know, but it's not common knowledge. And the fact that nobody knows this stuff hides the brilliance of humanity. Instead, they think some banker on Wall Street is brilliant because he figured out how to make a lot of money.

People's senses got so twisted. They think they need money, more than water. They want toxin more than medicine. It makes it very difficult to understand how to engage with the universe, or the reality, right?

Yeah I mean, when you think about the universe, the fact that you can make a lot of money means nothing! These people finding water: that's universal.

And the Wall Street guys just take drugs and watch TV, to avoid reality. Or they kill themselves. It's almost like this civilization has lost its drive to live. Does that go back to the one problem that you were talking about?

Rather than solve a problem, this culture has in fact become a problem. It's not that global warming is the problem. A virus isn't the problem. *We* are the problem because we provoked those things to manifest. This culture is the problem. The culture, the way of life, whatever term you want to use. And until we recognize that, we're not going to solve the real problem. Until we're able to say, we have lost the ability to fit with nature, so that we have become in fact outside of nature, and so in fact we have become the problem.

It's like we're alienated, we're disconnected from that life force. Or how do you think about it?

Well, that's who we are. We're that life force. That's what we are. We're like the virus saying "they got a vaccine to kill us, but we're gonna fight it, we're gonna find a way to survive." It's the same with all life, throughout the universe. All living things strive to live.

So striving to live is a sort of resistance?

Yes, it's a resistance. Resisting the death that's before it. And that's what our generation, our culture, our consciousness should be. The will to live.

constantly changing
many bodies/one spirit
in/out-one breath
many drums/one rhythm
rural/earth
city/cement
San Francisco east/ New York west
families separated by space yet together
we are one life- one energy
living to create
love/tribe/family- one hip people
Moving together thru one environment
We begin the consciousness of the future/present

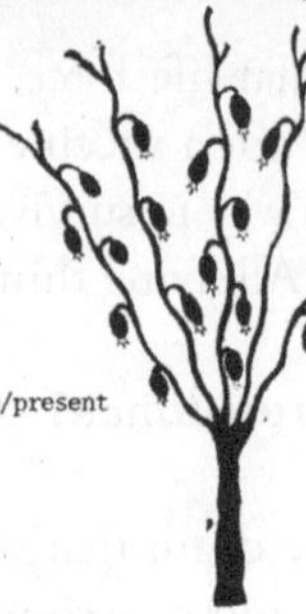

Community: The collection of families, communes, and tribes within one local geographical space. Tribal council; expanded family in control of environment. The local possibility for total life.

Family: the new reality - our base for existence on a day to day level. The least destructable unit. A group of people coming together out of love and trust - not compulsive like the bourgeoise family - a merging of individual energies becoming one strength, altering all weaknesses. Each being stands separately, but not alone.

People: The national collection of tribes/communities. The tribal-nation. The identity as a people. The merging with the cities and the country. The realization of the urban/rural struggle and the need for flow between them. As people we abolish space and time. We are one wherever we go. The highest form of communal existence: total environment. The creation of our [illegible] life, culture, destiny. The revolutionary alternative The new within the old The seed within the shell The form for creation and the vehicle for defense. The armed hip alternative. The new culture and the destruction of the old. The foundation of our vision and its realization.

Tribe:

expanded family
connected bands of consciousness
mobility-interchange
those who realize a similar identity

New Voices:

"Brothers and sisters of the revolt world:

They talk about our people and our world. They don't realize about themselves. Its no peace in our world like living together, like getting stoned and talking to each other on the streets without getting continuous brutality from the pigs. What the revolt-world needs is to get together like families of people so they can understand eachothers feelings and think very much of the revolt struggle for freedom."

THE MOTHERFUCKERS   UAW ARMED LOVE MF

DAY TWELVE

We've reached a point in the story where you came out of the wilderness, and you're starting to encounter these other worlds. We respect your decision not to reveal certain details. Are there any subjects you'd rather we avoid?

No. The things that I'm reluctant to reveal, I won't mention.

So what did you do when you left the wilderness? How did you handle coming back?

You know how deep sea divers come up slowly, they can't come up all at once. It was like that. When we came down from the wilderness, we didn't come down immediately to civilization, so to speak. We were still in a rural, high elevation, we stayed in the foothills and homesteaded. So it wasn't a total culture shock.

You'd been alone for a long time right?

I was never alone, I was with my wife.

I mean but you two were alone. Or I guess sometimes you met people, when you were in the wilderness?

It varied. Sometimes other groups would camp with us, or people would join us to ride with us for a little while. Most of the time, it was her and I.

Then gradually you moved from nomadic, horseback life, to more settled.

I always used the word "homestead." In other words, I built a house. I built a little cabin out of logs. And we had a garden, we had animals, we kept livestock. So that we were self-sufficient.

You built your house yourself?

Well I wasn't a carpenter, but logs I could figure out. You take a log and you cut a notch on either end, and then you stack them together. It's pretty simple. That's why people built log houses. You don't have to be technically proficient, you just have to be willing to struggle with it. I cut the logs in the mountains and hauled them down by hand. It was a beautiful little cabin.

It must be very cold country, lots of snow in the winter?

Yeah, winter's cold. I've seen it go 30, 40 degrees below zero. And I've seen lots of snow. One time we got five feet of snow in one weekend. Five feet! But generally, you manage. Even when it gets super cold, or there's a lot of snow, it's only a few days, you know.

Did you use firewood for heat?

Firewood yeah, that's all we had for heat. We had a wood stove. We didn't have running water, we hauled water and filled a big barrel by the house. I mean it was pretty primitive. We never did what most Americans would consider normal, like indoor plumbing and central heat.

Were there other people that homesteaded with you?

On our land, there were three families. My wife and I, and two other families that shared the land with us. Each had their own home, we weren't a commune. But we all lived on the same land, and shared everything. We did farming, and making crafts together, we did everything together. And we worked together, the three men worked as lumberjacks. That's why I was able to cut my own logs and build a house.

How did you come to settle there? You just took over the empty land?

No, we knew the people who owned the land. They gave us permission to occupy it, so to speak. So we developed, we built everything ourselves, all the buildings for the livestock. We had goats and pigs so we built barns, we had chickens, we built a chicken house, we built all the sheds. We built our own environment.

When you started homesteading, that was before you had become part of Native communities?

It all happened together. When we were in the mountains on horseback, that was exclusive, we couldn't do other things as well. We couldn't travel by vehicle, we just lived with the horses. But when we homesteaded, we had a car and we could go to different reservations, we got involved with different Native communities, we started adopting kids — it all happened parallel around the same time.

You adopted many kids?

We raised forty kids! I'm like the old man in the shoe!

Just you and your wife? The two of you raised forty kids?

Yeah but some for shorter times, as was needed. We would take kids that were in need. And some were older, like teenagers. And they would take care of each other.

So you made a kind of community with your kids. Did you all live in the same house?

We had 350 acres! We had livestock, horses, I mean we had a regular ranch.

That was in Colorado?

Correct.

Wow, I knew that you had a lot of kids. But I imagined maybe you supported some of them, but didn't live with all of them.

No, they all lived at the ranch. But that gave them something to do! They would take care of the animals, they would go collect the eggs, they'd help with the garden…I mean it was a whole life. And we had so much space so sometimes, we would have kids that would want to come for the summer, so we built an outdoor kitchen, we had tents and teepees, and kids would come stay. They would run around, do the chores with the farm animals, you know, they had a way of life. Some kids would only stay for the summer, but some then would want to stay longer, so they'd stay on and we'd put them in school, you know, it depended.

The kids themselves decided.

Right. And sometimes we took in really young kids, like one boy we adopted when he was four days old. I had a niece, a Native woman that I'd adopted as a niece, and she called me from the hospital and said she had a baby, and we should come get it. My wife and I tried to talk her out of it, like it might be good for her to raise a child, maybe it would help her. She was alcoholic. But she said "I won't do it, if you don't take the baby I'm gonna give it up for adoption." So we went to the hospital and we brought the baby home. And we raised him.

The kids were mostly Native American, or Mexican American, or white, or...?

Most of them are Native and Mexican mixed. And most were in need, like from dysfunctional families, so we would take them in. Some we kept for a year or two years, some less than a year, some their whole lives. So it would all vary.

You didn't treat it as a political project, or like an institution you could get funding for, or something like that?

No. It was completely self-regulated and self-financed. Just us. And I worked, I was making money. I made a lot of money as a lumberjack. You know, it's dangerous work. I lost my hearing, I'm deaf in one ear because of it. I cut my leg with a chainsaw, now I walk with a cane. I had trees dropped on my head. I mean it's dangerous. It's probably one of the most dangerous jobs that exists.

It's like you were saying about the Pancho Villa syndrome, you couldn't just become a dentist. You needed intensity.

Right. It's like the deep sea divers, they come up slowly. I had to go slowly from living with danger every minute, to partial danger. Then finally after many years I could handle no danger. It took a long time.

You had a big crew that you worked with?

Well it depends on the size of the job. There were a core of us that would work together. But like one year we cut firewood, so we had two people running saws and one splitting. We cut twenty-four tons of firewood that season! Some years we had contracts to build corrals for people, or to clear the way for roads, you know it changed every year. So we had different crews. Sometimes we'd have like ten people working together, and they all lived there at the place, we'd be together all the time.

So you very deliberately chose this group of people that you worked with.

Yeah, they were people we were associated with. We didn't advertise or hire people.

Were there some people still with you from the city, like older political relations?

No. Some were Native ceremonial people that I knew from that world. A lot of them were from different reservations. But there was no older political…For forty years I pretty much stayed away. And off the grid.

Did you have access to information, like if revolutions or uprisings were happening, were you getting information like that?

Yeah I tried to keep up with the news of what was going on. But I didn't remain visible in a political struggle. Life was a struggle, and building a community, and raising these kids. To me that was the struggle.

Do you know who Wilhelm Reich was? The psychoanalyst. Originally he was a student of Freud, but he broke with Freud. It's hard to paraphrase in one sentence, you know, he wrote lots of books, but basically he felt that it was an error to concentrate on the mind. He felt that the mind and body work together, and that you could reach the body more easily than the mind. So he tried to understand how the body is restricted in this society. He was very political. He didn't want to use psychoanalysis just to help people with their problems. He wanted to solve problems in society.

Anyway I first got interested in Reich when I was in the prison hospital, I started reading his work. I got pretty familiar with it. And he wrote a book that influenced me tremendously, called *The Murder of Christ.* Basically what he was saying is that Christ made a mistake by allowing himself to become a martyr, and then to be used by what he called the plague, the authoritarian structure. He said that instead of going to Jerusalem to become a martyr, Christ should have taken this understanding that he'd reached and gone into the mountains, amongst the people, and shared that. And that thought really affected me. Because I could see that I was on this suicidal, martyr path. It was clear. If I continued what I was doing in my political active life…I'd already been earmarked for elimination. And so I thought of what Reich was saying. It became a metaphor for me, like I had a choice to remain and become a martyr, or to go out and try to find ways to help people and break from this society. So rather than remaining a political activist on the road to martyrdom, I was trying to share with people, to build a way of life that's free of the authoritarian structure. Outside of it. To build some alternative way. And so that became the struggle.

When you left the city, you already had this vision of going to the mountains. That also saved your life in a sense.

Right. Then once we came out of the wilderness, and we had the homestead, we had all this land, we had a farm, we started taking in kids — it became a chance to realize that vision.

But it's interesting because what you did in the Lower East Side, you were also taking in kids and runaways. You continued in a sense.

We continued in a different manner. Like in the city, we had crash pads. So we would find kids in the street that had run away, and we'd tell them where there was a crash pad. And somebody older would be there, you know, we took turns. It wasn't that we had one home and they all came to our home. We would have multiple crash pads. So the method changed, but the effort was similar.

You know, some were really young kids, like 10 years old, 12 years old. We'd see them in the street and ask them, "you got any place to stay?" And we'd give them an address where to go stay. So we took care of them. Protected them too. We had patrols at night walking around looking for the kids, making sure they were alright; we had our own street patrol. We had doctors and lawyers, we had clothing at the free store, we had free food. We used to get day-old food from the markets, we had papers from a liberal church and we'd go to the vegetable market, and the meat and fish markets, we'd get enough to feed four or five hundred people. Then different people would cook, like there were some street people that had a history of cooking, and they would take over the cooking. We would have big meals two or three nights a week, in the Lower East Side. And so we did the same thing in the rural area but in a different way, in a different environment.

Last time I met with you just by myself, you told me a lot of interesting stories about the family. First you were close with Living Theater people, and then you started gathering all different groups of people, theater people, people from Bookchin's group, students from SDS, all these different groups.

We attracted them and they would join us. Two or three from all these different groups.

Maybe because they saw the richness of your community building, that's why they all respected you. These houses you opened to kids, and the community activities, creating common life in this urban context. I don't know if other groups were able to do that.

And the ones that came with us, you know, it wasn't a unified approach. There was no demand like "you have to move in with us." It wasn't a commune. It was an effort to change life. So there were some people that had homes with their families, they wouldn't give up their family life but they would come and be around with us, and share in that effort. Then there were some that had no home — their home was our home. They gave up their family life, to live this total communal life. But there was no demand, like "you have to leave your family and come with us." It was up to each person.

Whenever you want to come, come. And whenever you want to leave, leave.

Right. That's how it was. So people with nuclear families would be part-time participants in our world. They didn't give up their separate lives.

A lot of people did leave their homes and live together?

Yeah especially if they were unattached. Generally those who were a couple that had kids, they would remain…and yet come with us on other levels. Whereas most of the people in what we called the family were not couples. They would become couples sometimes, but they were more unattached.

So they're more open to different relationships, not like owning each other.

And this was the '60s, you know, there was an effort to break this attachment consciousness. It's an effort that couldn't be fully realized, but there was this instinct.

In other words, the core group of the family was committed to each other. Your identity with the family was more important than your identity as a couple.

Most of the family were men?

No it was both, men and women.

Right but I mean like in the core group, it seems like the majority were men?

It was both. Women were an essential part of it. What the family was, could not have been without them.

How about kids? There were runaways, but no one with their own kids?

Well nobody with a nuclear family really lived in our environment. There was one couple that did for a while, but it didn't last. It didn't work for them. You know and I could understand it, people have a sense of creating a home for their family. I mean that's instinctual. It's the nesting instinct, all humans have it.

And so that becomes somewhat of a conflict. Because the effort we were making as a family had an altruistic undercurrent — it was an effort to change society. So that took precedence over trying to find a life that satisfies you. It's not sustainable, if your main effort is to have a little family.

Also because it was dangerous, like you said, you were ready to risk your life.

And you can't force someone, you can't say that one is more important than the other. It depends, it's up to each person.

Like to me, as a person, my objective was change. That was my personal objective. To change the world. That took precedence over anything else.

You were a revolutionary. That was your basic existential imperative.

I was a true radical! My whole objective was change. It still is, actually.

DAY THIRTEEN

Ben, we're excited to go on with the story. But first, if you don't mind, I'd like to go back a little bit.

Well sure. Where do you want to go?

You told us about the book that influenced you by Wilhelm Reich, *The Murder of Christ*. But your first encounter with Reich was actually in the prison hospital, you said?

Right. When I was younger, and I was a drug addict. I was addicted to heroin. And one time I was in jail, and my liver gave out. I had severe hepatitis, I was dying. So they put me in a prison hospital. And while I was in there, I had access to books, I had therapy, you know. That's where I started painting! And that was where I first encountered Reich.

So you read that book already when you were in there?

No, but I started reading Reich and understanding what he was talking about, how the body had been controlled and structured. And afterwards I kept looking into his work, I came across that one. I can't remember when exactly. But I came to it before I went into the mountains. It became a metaphor for the choice I faced: to remain and become a martyr, or go out and build something.

That was a diverging point from your old comrades, who were into what you call the Pancho Villa syndrome.

Right. Exactly.

Your time in the prison hospital was really transformative, that you encountered these things.

Totally. That was how I started painting. There was a therapist that took an interest in me, and she really tried to help me. She started me painting as therapy. Sixty years later, I'm still painting!

Painting has been very important for your existence, mind and body.

Yeah! It was part of my restructuring. I left the world of hard drugs, I quit heroin. And I gravitated to the expansive psychotropic and psychedelic elements, like in the beginning LSD, or mescaline or psilocybin. I really believed, and I still believe, that we are completely structured by society. Some people used the term "brainwashed." But it's not just our brain, it's our whole being! I was friends with Tim Leary, and I believed, like Timothy was saying, that LSD will rewire you. I used it, and it did, in a sense. Then eventually I moved away from chemicals like LSD, towards organic psychotropics. But in the beginning I was involved with LSD, to restructure.

After all, LSD wasn't as helpful as it first seemed?

I wouldn't say that it wasn't helpful. But it was no longer necessary for me. Maybe it was important at some moment, and I got the benefit of it. I rewired to a degree where I could find a way out. And so then I went in the direction of Indigenous people who use psychotropic plants. There are all different kinds. Some cultures used wine, some used hashish, some used psilocybin, or like *yage* or *ayahuasca* in the Amazon. People found things that would help them communicate with something outside of themselves.

Outside of the social infrastructure.

Right. That's where the commonality with Reich comes in. His work was all about structure, how the authoritarian structure physically impairs the ability to flow. He tried to understand this, to find ways to break free from it. Indigenous people understood it without the theory of it. They understood that certain plants, like a lot of Native American cultures use tobacco...So many different things have been used to go beyond.

But while you were in New York, you were using LSD.

Correct. I never used it after I left New York.

For you that was also part of the political struggle, to break this structuring.

And as I was restructuring, or reinventing, I was entering a wider field. I came to see that politics was limited. You don't want to just change the ruler, you want to change the need to be ruled. So that is internal as well as external. You have to change the need to be ruled. It's almost impossible to explain it.

So that became my next journey. When I left New York, I left street activism, I left LSD, I left those things that had been needed in the city to break. Then I had to find the alternatives to that, once I'd made the break.

I'm curious how LSD stopped being useful for you, exactly.

You know, LSD is really heavy. And at some point, you're rewiring and you broke from that, there's no need to keep breaking. Now's the time to go toward rebuilding. I had to find a way…and part of it was entering the wilderness, where I could become communicative with the elements. I lived with them. When I would hunt, it wasn't like I'm hunting this animal, it's like we're sharing, we're living together. And I have to ask permission to take its life, to continue my living. It's not just me, we're there together. We have a life built on each other.

So they become part of you.

And in turn you become part of them. I have never been able to explain it, most people don't understand these things. Yet. Maybe someday.

But in a certain sense people used to understand it?

They totally understood it! At some point. Before Western civilization.

Even in Buddhism there's this idea, you eat plants and fish and animals, but when you die you give your body back to them. It's a good thing to be eaten.

Right. And I always felt that it would be easier for people from non-Western cultures to understand, because they don't have to go as far back. Western culture has to go way back! They lost this understanding a long time ago. Whereas like Buddhism or other cultures kept certain elements. And that's why I always felt more attracted to other cultures. I was never attracted to the Western culture.

Like jazz, that was a big influence in your early life.

It was an influence then, and it still is. My whole life up until now has never been European — that's a small part. Black culture was a big part when I was growing up. Native American culture is a big part now. And continually Black culture. My spirituality is connected to Asian influences, like Zen, and Tantric traditions. I mean there's so much non-European in my make-up.

But it's significant that you were also influenced by Reich in a substantial way.

You know, I'm criticizing Western culture, obviously. But there are certain things, like for me, Reich is really important. Einstein's theory of relativity is really important, and the concept of the unified field. I really build my personal philosophy on that concept, that life is one. That's really Tantric. They understood that way before Einstein was born: the connection of the human to this universe.

Einstein discovered mathematical formulae. But as a perception, people from different cultures understood it way before.

Thousands of years! For thousands of years, Indigenous people have understood their connection. To everything. They're not above it, they're part of it. Whereas Western culture puts man at the pinnacle, above.

Like in ancient Egypt, way back, before it was Muslim, they had the idea of the scarab. You know what a scarab is? It's a beetle, iridescent green. It's beautiful. And it's a dung beetle. You know what dung is? It's shit! And that meant something to them, that here's this most beautiful beetle, coming from shit. That's some consciousness that the West doesn't grasp!

That's a beautiful example.

There's so much out there that the "modern man" is ignorant of.

I see what you mean about why it's hard to explain, because what you're talking about, like when you're hunting

and living with the deer, it's not just a matter of thinking about it. Your senses, your perception, everything must have changed. So you're living together in awareness and shared realms of sensibility with the deer and everything.

Right. It's not just a thought. It's a reality, it's physical.

The body is really part of the Earth. But in modern capitalist life it's hard to understand that. What I'm doing is increasingly detached from my own body, without understanding what's happening here, in relationship with the planet. So in a sense what you've been doing is to recover this relationship. Through animism you try to recover this body and Earth relation.

In reality, your body is a universe. What exists in the universe actually is what your body is. The way things move in your body. Like nobody even thinks of that anymore. They only think about what you're doing *with* your body, that superficial "what you're doing." They don't think about what you *are*.

Once, people tried to understand their place. There was some thought about the human's place in the universe. But now everything is technological, cell phones, social media. Nobody thinks anymore about the larger picture. They're all thinking about these tools, it's no longer contextual. And so it's even harder now. It's gotten worse and worse, in the modern era. Everything's entrenched.

More and more detached.

Right. Alienation. I mean there's people sitting on social media for ten hours a day. And you have no room to think. There's no need to think, because it's all there for you. So whatever the problems had been before are exacerbated, they're even worse now.

People in general are made to live in this way. They go to the bank and withdraw cash, send text messages, go to work and type words into the computer, that's their life. It's all signs, it's all semiotic. They're not aware of the air, or like the energy between you and me, you know?

That's why, I think we talked one time about the problem of entertainment. I really think that's a destructive element in capitalist society, that people want to be entertained. In other words, you're not participating in something creative for yourself, you're just observing. In Indigenous, pre-capitalist societies people did things themselves, they interacted. There was no sense of entertainment like "I'm gonna go watch these guys dance." They went and joined the dance.

It's not like you watch and there's an object of spectacle. You are part of it.

Like in the '60s, in Tompkins Square Park, Black street people would always bring drums and play together. I used to sit in with them, cuz you know I was a musician, I played the vibraphone which is a percussive. So I used to play drums with them in the park, we'd sit and play conga, like maybe six of us. We spent hours there, we would stand around playing, and somebody would be dancing in place, you know, it was an energy. That hardly exists anymore today.

Also in the jazz world when you were growing up, it was the same kind of thing right?

Yeah, we used to get together like in the school auditorium, they let us play there, or in church basements in the neighborhood.

The community provides these spaces for you.

Right. But that's all changed now because of the idea of entertainment. So I think that's important to differentiate, that in pre-capitalist culture there was no sense of entertainment.

With capitalism, music became an object of investment.

Exactly. But that's reduced our culture immensely! And I don't know if it's possible to ever go back to the full extent of Indigenous involvement in consciousness, but we could go partially back. In other words, reduce the idea of entertainment, and have more people making music together, not as entertainment but as a spiritual or aesthetic act. I think that's really important.

Instead of commodifying art, you want to encourage people's engagement in art. Not like these artists that hang their art in galleries in Chelsea and sell it for millions of dollars. They're more like money mongers than artists.

And even the word "artist" is an artificial word. What's essential is creativity, the expressive urge. Art is not a product: it's a way of expressing. It's like breathing. It's an essential part of human life. And that's what's been lost.

Indigenous pre-capitalist cultures all had art. But they didn't call it art. It was part of their life. Like if you look at the shelters of Indigenous people: I have seen some that are more magnificent than any architect ever designed. The word "art" is misleading...Say you make a post to hold something up. Well you carve the post. The post is not a sculpture. But it *is* sculpture. In other words, the art is included. They built their living environments in an artistic way. It's not the object, it's the expression.

It's like making a mark. I've used that term instead of "art." It's not that I'm producing art. I'm making a mark. That's what the human does. When they didn't even have language yet, they uttered sound. They'd walk around and find a bone, they'd pick up the bone and make a mark.

That's why I say that art is like breathing. You can't live without breathing. Well you can't live without art, without making a mark. It's not an object, it's a motion. It's living.

Motion. Relation. Relating yourself to the universe.

Right. It's a way the human says "I'm alive. I exist." And that expression of life is a necessity. Like Aboriginal people had to look for food almost twenty hours a day, and they still had time to make what we call art.

Think about it from an animistic understanding. You create because you are part of creation. If you sense there's this creation, that everything is alive and in motion and that life is moving in you, then art becomes a way for you to identify with it and to be part of it.

In other words, art is our entry. It's a way to connect with the greater whole.

SEE FLOW
IN
SOME-WAY
BREAK THROUGH
THE CUBED-ELECTRIC-CAGE
ILLUSION
(REALITY FLOWS
OUTWARD-ONWARD-INWARD)
COSMIC CONSCIOUSNESS SEES — THE EARTHLY NEEDS /
(GREATER MOVES THE STRENGTH)
CREATED ANEW
THE SEA / THE BLOOD /
THE BEATING HEART THE CHANGING BODIES
PULSE AND MOTION / THE FOOD, THE FISH
THE SEA THE AIR & WIND
CYCLONE FURY LIFTING US TO OUR
FUTURE VISION: THE LIBERATED
PLANET EARTH.
MOTHER-FUCKERS

DAY FOURTEEN

Today feels like a good day to ask: what is revolutionary animism? It's not like revolution in the conventional sense, I guess.

The problem is that people tend to think of revolution as an event. To me, revolution is not an event. It's a way of life. So the minute you realize that this life has to change, you have to start to change things in your daily life. It doesn't end there. I'm not a reformer. I'm not saying just change it in your life, and that's good enough. It's not good enough. But if you're waiting for the revolution to change it, it's not going to happen. You have to change it in your life. And the more people change it in their lives, the more it will change in all life.

From your experience of changing yourself and fitting into nature, becoming subservient to nature, what can you suggest for people who live in cities, or really anyone at this point? What else is there?

Well my belief is that, if you have an animist understanding, then you slowly alter the way you do things. I'll give you an example.

Like Indigenous people, when they took an animal's life, to them that was sacred. They took its life, and they used everything in that animal. They didn't waste anything. And people say "well you can't go back and be a hunter gatherer. "No, you can't. But you can take the principle, and follow it.

Take a simple thing, like electricity. Why overuse it? Why overuse anything? You have to see it on the small scale. You know, I don't have heat here, in this apartment. I don't need to. I don't want to contribute to the electric company. So I try to live without it. We all make choices on how to survive. We must continually make efforts. It sounds so simple, it's hard to convey…

It's almost the opposite of saying that people should try to go back.

You can't go back! But you look at other cultures and learn from them, try to understand what they had and bring it forward somehow. If there's a part that can help you, you try to understand it, and let it alter your way of life.

Like in this culture, people have gotten the idea that you must be comfortable. People are totally reliant on comfort. And that prevents you from doing certain things. You become dependent. It becomes a hindrance to a revolutionary life. It's like I told one of my grandsons. He's gone now, but I told him, "Grandson I'm gonna give you a sentence. If you follow this, you could do anything in life." He said "oh yeah what is it Grandpa?" I said, "be comfortable with discomfort. If you're comfortable with discomfort, you could do anything."

It may sound simplistic, but it's important. And that's apparent to me, that there are simple, everyday concepts that can be so important. But it's hard to explain to political people. You know, who cares about comfort?

It's actually very political, I mean the world is being destroyed because people want to drive expensive cars and

have a suburban house with a media room and a green lawn, all these everyday things are destructive.

And a lot of so-called revolutionaries think that revolution is an event. Well what if that event can't happen now? You might as well join the middle class, because you can't have the event? But if you understand that it's a way of life, then you must live in a revolutionary way, even if the revolutionary event can't happen yet. And if enough people do that, then maybe it will.

In other words, you don't believe in one big goal for revolution. It's not some ultimate event that makes everything better.

Right. There is no finality. It's a process. It doesn't end.

Another critique of Marxism is that it tried to set the course for revolution. Everything should be correct. No revolution happens that way.

Because they think their ideology is correct. And their effort is to bring everybody in line with their thought. As if reality should follow their thought. It's the same mistake as thinking that the human is in charge. Some people think the human is the pinnacle of life, and their effort is to bring everybody under their control. As if all the animals are just there for them to use. Who the hell do they think they are? The human is also an animal! Not better or worse.

Maybe worse at this point.

The human is just another animal. The universe is total, and the human is just a part of it. The human not the main character — it's a footnote! Barely a footnote.

Do you know the term "perspectivism"? Some anthropologists

use it to describe certain Indigenous worldviews that decenter the human perspective, by seeing that all life has perspective. Does that resonate?

I don't know enough about the use of that term, but I would reject it as too subjective. If it's your perspective then it's you're seeing, you're judging, you're thinking…In animism, your thought is not central. Animism means we don't care what you're thinking, the universe is moving! You can think anything you want.

And the emphasis on thinking is unimportant. You don't know how animals think, how nature put that process within them. It's not definable. They're not going to define it for you. And you can't define it because you're not them. So it's better to just see everything as part of it. You don't have to understand it. It doesn't care if you don't understand it! Who are you, anyway? Like, the universe! Do you have any idea how big the universe is? There are black holes out there devouring planets! While humans are talking about the importance of their thoughts.

I think your idea is a little similar to Buddhism.

I would go the opposite: Buddhism is similar to it. Animism came first. Animism was the original understanding of man. It wasn't just a thought, it was a way of being. Everybody on Earth was an animist. Whether they had a term for it or not, it doesn't matter. You don't have to talk about it. The fact that you are alive, you are carrying that energy that created you, so you are part of this creation. Whether you recognize it or not. The fact that you don't recognize it will give you a problem. The fact that you recognize it might help you a little.

In animism, of course plants and animals are living, but also minerals and stones and everything?

Everything. A stone isn't just sitting there stationary. There are elements within that are moving. They're spinning, things are in motion! Life is based on motion. It's like string theory. Forget the old image of the atom with the nucleus in the center and the electron particles. That's ancient history now. Instead of particles, there's these vibrating strings of energy. And that energy is more predominant than the material! Motion is the essence. That's what the universe is: total motion.

You don't think about it as energy, but motion.

Because with energy there's a source, and a result. Motion just is. It doesn't know you're looking at it, and it doesn't care. I'm moving! Get out of the way!

I like how you use science to talk about animism. But with others you've shared animism with, I assume not everyone talks about string theory and atoms.

No. Some of them probably never even used those terms.

Then I guess they use different metaphors?

Sure, everybody has their own metaphor. But the metaphor is not important. What they're talking about, that's important. Not how they define it. Or how they perceive it, or how they see it, or what perspective they have. It exists in spite of them. It exists. Period.

So that's the basic message, that there's existence outside of us.

Animism is not theology. It doesn't have an ideology. We don't care if you believe or don't believe. That's one problem with the concept of god as an anthropomorphic entity. If you think of god as an entity, then you have to choose: there is a god, or there is no god. But if you say there's no god, that means what? There's something. There's creation, there's nature, there's energy — it's all in motion. Nobody is directing it. You got black holes eating planets! And if your planet is the one caught, that's it, you're gone! There's not some entity out there saying "well, you shouldn't eat that planet."

It's important to understand that there are forces beyond our control. We are part of it, but we can't control it.

It's like a tsunami. You can't say "how can there be a just god that killed so many people in the tsunami." If you're in its path, the tsunami got you. There's no director, it's just moving. And that's the problem with the concept of god, if you think of it as a conscious being. It is not conscious. It's alive.

It's a pure life force.

Correct. It's not making judgment. Or, say you pray. You don't pray to it to help you because you think it will come and help you. No, you pray to it to help you, by putting yourself in its realm. It's not like the cosmos is going to stop doing what it does to help you. But by asking it for help, you're putting yourself in connection with it, and you'll find your help. Not through its intervention necessarily, but through connecting to it.

That's why prayer is essential. It's a way of directing energy. Like some Native people, they smoke. And they have a thought. And they're thinking this smoke is going to carry that thought. It's not about talking to a higher being.

It's not about consciousness, but connectivity.

It's trying to enter that realm…whatever that realm is. You don't have to define everything. In fact many Native people use the term "great mystery," which is so true. That's what it is, a great mystery. Nobody knows what it is. We can't know, and we don't need to know! Who are we? We just have to acknowledge that we're part of it.

That's where science is wrong. Science thinks it can find an answer to everything. There is no answer to everything. If you're looking for an answer to everything, you just wasted your time. There is no answer to everything. There's a feeling. You have to look for that feeling. It's a wonder…It's awe.

When it comes to the people that were elders to you, who could give you a kind of spiritual guidance – I don't know if that's the right word, obviously it's not a matter of them knowing something.

And teaching you something.

But it is a matter of them being, maybe, closer to that feeling?

That's it. Exactly. And they don't tell you. It's unspoken. You just watch and understand. The Western culture is enamored with words. They think words are so important. But they're not! The word could be your downfall. And words will not bring you to an answer. See, the universe is abstract. It is not possible to understand in an intellectual manner. It has its own way of being that you can't completely understand. It will always remain abstract.

Because it can't be conceived in terms of thinking? But what about experienced in terms of feeling, or intuition? Can't intuition communicate with abstraction?

But it cannot be infallible. In other words, you can't assume that you're correct. You have to just go with it. There's no way to say "oh yeah I'm right. I'll check off that box." I mean there's so many things in the universe that the intellectual mind could never understand. Like the universe doesn't have any sense of hierarchy or what's right. It's like this little ant is not inferior to this planet. It has no…You can't put a word to it.

And nobody understands how these things work. Like planets devour other planets. Are they absorbing the energy, are they eating the energy of this other planet? Is it obliterating them? Or is it just…And you don't even know if it knows. There's no knowing! And you have to accept that fact, that there's no knowing.

That's very brilliant. That's really philosophy. Ben Morea's philosophy.

I don't know if I want to accept that.

From what you're saying, if there's no knowing, are there even things? How would you know one thing from another thing?

The furthest I could go is to say that in animism, everything is connected. But you cannot say how it's connected. It's connected in the abstract sense. If you think of the universe as one, one entity, or one…you could almost say one body. It is one. It's like your body. You can say I have a heart, I have arms. But the body is a whole. And so the universe is a whole. And there are many universes, I mean there's millions. But it's still one. The human mind almost can't wrap around it. And you have to accept the fact that you can't understand it; you just have to find a working relationship with it. A way to treat it, a way to think of it. You can't really understand its essence, what it is.

Think of this: they talk about the big bang. But did they ever say what it is that's supposed to be banging? How was there a big bang, if there was nothing to bang? So when you say "big bang" you can understand that something collided, and created the universe. But you'll never understand how something could collide, if there was nothing to begin with. Nothing doesn't collide with nothing! But they never talk about that. They can't admit it.

They want to think there's a beginning, that's the problem.

If you force the idea that there should be a beginning, then you need this kind of explanation.

How could there be a beginning, when there was nothing to begin! See that's why the abstract is so important. It's not a matter of intellectually understanding, but rather feeling, just trying to connect.

This is a random question but, what about your dreams?

Dreams are extremely important. But it's the kind of thing you can't put terminology to. I would never say it's another dimension, I wouldn't define it like that. I don't know how, if the mind receives certain information, or how it happens. But dreams are important. They're real. I can't say how, or why. But they're as real as you and I sitting here like this.

Like one time, we were living in the mountains, and we were out of food. I was always hunting, obviously. Generally I went hunting for large game like deer or elk. So I would go out in the morning, and my initial effort was to look for large game. But if I didn't get anything, then sometimes coming home I would look for small game, so that at least we could eat dinner. I had a shotgun and it used two kinds of shot: little BBs for small game, and solid bullets for large game. So I would change the shot depending on what I was hunting.

So I'd been out for a few days in a row hunting, and hadn't caught anything. And I had a dream. In my dream I saw a hill in front of me, and there was a deer on top of the hill. It was looking at me, and I thought "shit, there it is." Then I realized I had those little BBs in the shotgun. I couldn't shoot it! And the deer left. It kind of looked at me, and left.

That morning, I woke up and I thought "oh boy, I had that dream. I'm gonna switch it around." Usually I put the BBs in when I was coming home, so I figured that I must have been on my way back when I saw the deer. And I thought, "I'm gonna fool the dream. I'm gonna do the opposite. I'll put the BBs in first, and I'll come back with the bullets." Because I was taking the dream as real. So I went out. It was still early in the day. And I saw a hill in front of me, just like in my dream. It was the same hill! And there was a deer on top of the hill. The same deer. And it looked at me, and I said, "oh shit! I got the little BBs in here, I can't shoot it!" The deer just looked at me, and left.

It was exactly like the dream! The same hill, the same deer — exact! That's how real dreams can be.

It's not just a freaky occurrence. A dream is a real thing. That's what you want to say, right?

Yeah. And I can't say how. Or why. It's real though.

Then I guess you shouldn't interpret your dreams? Or I wonder what you thought.

I thought I tried to fool the dream, but the dream fooled me.

So no more trying to fool the dream after that. You have to take it straight?

Well I don't know what the lesson is. It just showed me that dreams are real. I mean it was the exact hill! The exact deer, the way it was standing. Everything was the same.

DAY FIFTEEN

If you think back to childhood, can you recall some early awareness of being revolutionary? Like a first moment when you sensed that this fucked-up reality needs to be changed?

Like a bright spot, or a light bulb?

Well it doesn't have to be that dramatic, but yeah.

You know, as I was growing up, as a teenager, my mother used to say to me, "I can't figure out what I did wrong that makes you the way you are, so negative about this world. I must have done something wrong." She used to say that all the time. So it must have been obvious to her that I was not satisfied. But I can't say it happened one particular moment. It's just, that's how I was.

You remember that Japanese woman Yuri Kochiyama, that we talked about a while back? She lived near me when I was growing up. We lived in the same housing project in Hell's Kitchen. And the majority of the people in this project were not white, they were Black and Latino, you know, white was a minority. But she and I both lived there. And I often thought about it, and can never remember, when did I first meet her, or how? At some point I became conscious of her. And she was always observing me, like she would talk to me, you know, she was really sweet to me. I was young.

You were a teenager, right?

Yeah. I had moved there when I was 10. And I left when I was 17. So maybe I was 13 or 14. I don't know when exactly. And I don't know how she noticed me, but she was always really friendly. I often thought about it, I wonder why? And I came to the conclusion, I don't know if it's correct, but I thought that she was fascinated by the fact that I was totally at home with Black and Latino kids. That's who I played with, like that's all I was with. And maybe that's what caught her attention, that here's this little white kid here totally at home in the ghetto. Or, I don't know, I'm putting words in her mouth.

Maybe she was like you too, as a Japanese woman.

Right. I think it made an impression on her because she was that way also. I don't know how she ended up living there, in the project. Do you know anything about her family, was she married?

I believe that she and her family were put into an internment camp in California when she was young. And she became politicized during that time. Then later she did a lot in solidarity with the Cuban revolution, and Black struggles. I'm not sure if she was married.

See the reason I ask is because originally, when the projects were built, they were for veterans. So her husband might have been in the service. Like, my stepfather had been in the service. And it was really low-rent, so poor people were happy to have it, and people coming out of the military with no income gravitated there. But I don't know her family.

You also knew Yuri in a political context, you said you used to go to her house for meetings?

Correct. Years later, after I left the project, I met her again. She had moved uptown to Harlem somewhere. I don't remember where we met. But she remembered me, and she invited me to her home. I used to go up there when they were having meetings, or discussion groups, with Black militants and intellectuals, she would invite me. Everyone was Black except for me and her.

So I used to go to these meetings. And there was a person there that I really didn't get a good vibe from. Something didn't seem right, like he was too eager to please. And he would talk to me and try to find out more...Something just bothered me. Well it turned out that this person was a cop, or an informant. And he got people from that discussion group involved, he set them up — that's the terminology you use now, I didn't realize then — but they were gonna blow up the Statue of Liberty. And there was a big arrest, there were headlines everywhere, like "Black Militants Plot to Blow Up the Statue of Liberty." It was a way of putting a negative imprint on Black militancy. Those people got like twenty, thirty years in prison. And this guy set the whole thing up! He used to try to talk to me. I didn't trust him at all, so I would just kind of "yes" him to death, but I would never get involved. But I didn't know enough to say to Yuri, "hey I don't trust that guy." Because I was a guest there, and who am I to say that, and maybe I'm wrong or, you know, I was young. But I had a bad feeling.

Also it was at a time when, a few years later, COINTELPRO and the extent of infiltration would have been more clear.

A few years later I would have realized this guy is dangerous. And not only that, this man was her friend. He had really gotten in with her. He did things with the kids, he was like a part of the family. She'd completely bought into it. So I didn't want to insult her. And at the time I didn't know if I was making wrong assumptions, or if I had the wrong feeling. But my instinct was, this guy can't be trusted.

But that instinct, or I don't know what to call it, but I've had that throughout my life. Like one time I was with my wife — she wasn't my wife at the time, actually we never married, but she was my companion — anyway she and I were walking around in the Lower East Side. And all of a sudden I had this sense. I saw a cop car way up the street. You could hardly see it, it was about a block or two away. I stopped walking and I told her, "wait." See there was this one cop that was really trying to bust me, he was always following me, you know. And I could feel that he was there, in that car. My wife said "how could you possibly know that? It's two blocks away!" I said "he's in that car. I can tell." So she said "you stay here, I'm gonna walk by the car." She went across the street and walked up past the police car, went around and came back. She said "you know, he's in that car."

I could *feel* it. Like in the air. And I've always had that second sense. People that came around that were trying to set things up, or that were not correct politically, or legally, I always had that sense. And I relied on it. Like I told my wife, "he's in that car." I didn't say "I think," or "it may be." I said "he's in that car." It's not just me. People should be aware of it. There's something in the air, you have to attune yourself to it. It's there. In other words, people should be conscious of what's around all the time. Especially militant people.

Like another time, there was a demonstration and I was walking with my wife. And all of the sudden the cops charged it. I mean really violently. My wife got terrified, so I told her "let's go, let's turn down this corner." And then a cop came around the corner, pointing a gun. So I told her "don't panic. Don't even notice it. Make believe it's not there. Just keep walking nonchalant, like you're out for a stroll. Don't give any sign of fear." That's how dogs are: if you show fear they can feel it. And so we just walked, and this guy had his gun out, but we acted like we were strolling. And nothing happened.

These stories are a reminder of the danger you were living through back then. You really had to be sharp all the time.

All the time.

And your group was a pretty high profile target. You must have been extremely security conscious.

Always. I'll show you an example. Say you need to write somebody's phone number down. You have a system, nobody else knows it. Maybe you reverse the numbers, or you subtract one from each number, or whatever. You do whatever you're gonna do, but nobody else knows it. You never write a real number down. And like many people in our family, in the core group, had a friend that was not really political, someone who was sympathetic but not politically active. Everybody had somebody like that, and they would set up a safe deposit box. And there would be stuff in that safe deposit box that you could access, because you had the key.

It must have been hard to be in that heightened state, where you have to constantly be reading everything for danger.

It's actually not hard if you do it. It becomes a procedure, it's like part of your life. You're always setting up different safeguards.

But wasn't it hard on your relationships with each other, like the suspicion or paranoia?

Well I don't like to make categorical statements. But as far as I can tell, we may have been one of the only political groups in America that was never infiltrated. The way we operated, it was not possible. Because we weren't an organization. We were a family.

It's not like a meeting once a week or something, you were living together. And existentially, you know each other.

Right. And that was the era when infiltration was at a maximum. Everybody was infiltrated!

Can I ask you a question about being armed? You told us that you needed guns in everyday operation. So what divides those people that have guns and are ready to use them, from those who are radical but don't use guns?

Being armed, you have a consciousness of it. For instance if I went to a demonstration, I would not have arms. You have to know when to have them. And when you have them, you have to act accordingly. You have to be conscious.

Like one time we bodyguarded for the Panthers. They were doing a talk in the East Village and they contacted me and asked if we would come. They couldn't be armed themselves, you know, because of who they were. Also it was New York. So they asked if we could come be around the stage and act as guards.

Or like Malcolm X, he had people. He had two armed guards, they were like private detectives or whatever. They were always around him when he spoke in public. But there was an informant, somebody in his organization got the guards arrested. And that's when Malcolm got shot. The night they killed Malcolm, the guards were not there.

Somebody should have covered for him. Somebody's radar should have gone off and said "look, they arrested those two guys that protect him. Maybe we should cancel this night, or maybe we should get other people." But somebody dropped the ball and didn't warn him.

The people around him were not really aware of these things, maybe.

But he was such a high priority target, I mean somebody should have immediately thought "wait a minute, the two bodyguards were just arrested." Like someone overseeing security should have realized, "the guards are gone, so what do we do?" That would've been the first thing I would've done. The minute it happened, I would've said "there's something wrong. This is not right."

But, we're all human, sometimes we drop the ball. So maybe I'm talking in hindsight.

It's interesting how you talk about your group as a family. There's a sense of total loyalty almost like a traditional family, or even like the mafia kind of family. But it's not hierarchical or authoritarian. This idea of family seems really important.

And that's why we couldn't be infiltrated. Because we were a family. We weren't an organization, there was no way to join it. You're either part of it, or you're not. If somebody came and asked "can I join" — there's nothing to join. But say somebody comes and stays around, and you watch them for a few weeks, a few months, and they become part of it. Or they don't. But there's no way to join. So a person can't join and infiltrate it. You have to be part of it. And then you're not an infiltrator.

It's very intuitive, or organic.

It's both. But really, I never admitted it but, I was the engineer of that whole thing.

How did you know? I mean how did you come up with it?

I have no idea. But nobody else in our family had that understanding. It wasn't that two or three of us created it.

But it's really powerful, where that came from. Like from you, but bigger than that, you know.

It's probably a mixture of things. And I'm sure a lot of it has historical precedents. Throughout the world bands of people got together and created new subcultures, so to speak. Like the Merry Men in England, you know Robin Hood and those people. It's not just a story, they really existed. There were hunters and gatherers throughout England living in the forests, like they had a separate life. And they created a subculture, that was against the aristocracy. They banded together to move against the aristocracy.

Or like you mentioned the mafia. You know how the mafia started? The French occupied Italy. They controlled part of Italy. And the mafia started as a revolutionary group to fight for independence, to get rid of the French. And then became criminal — it's the Pancho Villa syndrome! But in some ways, the mafia was the peasant class fighting against the aristocracy. It wasn't just "criminal."

That happens everywhere, throughout history. Bands of people get together and form subcultures against domination.

DAY SIXTEEN

Ben, as much as we're inspired by our conversations, to be honest it's hard to think about what we can do today, in the current state of the world. Every week there's some new horrible news, and increasingly it seems that nothing is possible. And the more we read the more we're incapacitated, caught in a vicious cycle of the over-informed. So then there's nothing to do, you know?

Yeah, you feel overwhelmed. But you can't allow that. You have to just do what you can do, and feel out where you fit. What's possible. Like in the '60s, we were heavy into the struggle against the Vietnam War. To think about America, the most powerful nation at the time, that we could in any way affect what they were doing — that could've overwhelmed us. We could've said "oh well, what can we do." But we just said "no, we're gonna change it." That's the end of that. And we fought them like they were vulnerable. We didn't feel frightened. We felt like "we're gonna do it, or we'll die." But we're gonna try. And it takes that kind of risk...It's almost suicidal.

You fought the State like it was vulnerable, like it was susceptible to attack?

Yes. Not because we thought that we would be victorious. But because we felt like "we have to do something. Whether or not we're successful."

We were ready to confront the powers that be. But at the same time, I began to sense that the political struggle, by itself, was not enough. We had believed that it was, but I could see that it wasn't. The struggle was even greater than we'd realized. And that's the challenge today. We reached a point where people are really ready — if there's a fuller understanding — I believe there's a chance to bring people together. But politics alone is not enough. There has to be another dimension.

And that's where, to me, the spiritual element is crucial. I don't know about the 1800s, or the 1920s, or even the 1960s. But right now I can say that, if there's not some spiritual consciousness to the struggle, it's not going to happen.

You told us how you came to animism when you went out west. But how about when you were still in New York, did you have an idea of spirituality then?

Well, it was in my mind. I used to think all the time about the history of spiritual warriors, like the Bhagavad Gita, or like samurai. I felt that there was something…but I didn't understand it. And I started using Native designs because I sensed that Native people understood this other dimension. I wasn't clear about their spirituality, or how to define it. I didn't know how to talk about it. But I thought about it all the time. Then when I had to leave New York, I said to myself, "now is my chance." I wanted to find out what it was that I'd been thinking about, but couldn't understand.

There's something already unique about your thoughts, that you were connecting militancy to this traditional warriorship. You sensed some kind of cultural importance within the warrior tradition. Something beyond soldiers shooting guns.

Oh, way beyond!

You wanted to be more like a warrior, rather than just a killing machine.

I didn't want to be a soldier. There's a big difference. And I understood that Native people were warriors. They weren't soldiers. The technology that the soldiers had was so powerful, it eventually vanquished Native resistance. But the warrior had this tremendous energy. And you start to understand it was only because they couldn't match the firepower that they weren't victorious.

Did you ever hear of Dog Soldiers? That was a warrior society. They were Cheyenne, but they formed a separate society. They had stakes that they carried with them, and when they were overpowered, they would stake themselves to the ground. And they couldn't move from that spot.

It's like you were saying, there's a connection between the power to fight, and the willingness to lose your life.

And that was their way of life. They were so committed to that way of life, they would sacrifice their individual life for the tribe. And that was a source of tremendous power.

For you, maybe the warrior was essentially the same as the revolutionary?

No. They may coexist. But it's not an absolute.

But in some sense they seem similar. They're both ready to fight and die for something bigger than themselves.

Right, in some ways they may be very similar. But in other ways they could be totally different. For example, some revolutionaries are soldiers. Well, soldiers, when they're given an order, they're obligated to follow that order. But in Native cultures, you're not given orders. And if there's conflict, like say there's disagreement within a band or tribe: rather than fight against each other, one group might leave. For instance there was one tribe in Wyoming called Shoshone. At some point one group left, they went south. They moved into the southern plains, and they became known as Comanches. They were actually the same tribe! But they didn't wage war against each other. That's important to understand.

Yeah, that's a totally different paradigm. But it's fascinating that you had this conception of the spiritual warrior back when you were in the city. Like you're fighting cops and meanwhile you're thinking all the time about the Bhagavad Gita and stuff, right?

All the time. But I never talked about it. I kept it to myself. I didn't know how to talk about it because, in my mind, if you even mention the word "spirituality," you're gonna scare people away. Because they think of religion. Religion is so horrible, it destroyed spirituality.

Then eventually the word "spirituality" got co-opted by commercial movements. I mean it's a multi-billion dollar market now, especially so-called Eastern spirituality. But some of that really started in the '60s.

And in the West there's the idea that somehow spirituality means you don't defend yourself. It's absurd. Spirituality always had a defensive side. And that's what drew me, like I saw that, in my eyes, Native cultures had a warrior element and a spiritual element. They had both. These were people that would go to war to defend themselves, and still not be afraid to pray. And I wanted to understand how that was possible. We had the warrior part, but the spiritual part was missing. Like we dealt with art and politics, we thought both were necessary. But I always felt the lack of some other form of understanding.

I had this gnawing feeling that the political struggle alone was not sufficient. I really did. You can see, if you look at the posters I was making, there's a consciousness of another entity — I didn't completely understand it — but I was already feeling it out. Before it actually came to be. I had that premonition.

Yeah, that's premonition. Your visual work was a premonition.

Somehow I had this premonition that there was going to be more needed, because what we had was not enough. So I was laying out a path, so to speak. I didn't think about it like that at the time. But you could see that I was laying out a path, that the struggle had to expand into another dimension, in another direction. I want to show you something...Have you ever seen this book? It has a lot of the posters I made. See all these Native elements, like about the tree of life...Or this one, "know yourself, know your people." A Marxist would never do this! This was before I left the city. But you can see already, it was no longer the traditional political struggle.

This was all before you went out west.

Correct. So it's not like I went there and then all the sudden...This is what pushed me, partially. So that when it became a situation where I had to leave, I could see why, and where to go. I was already sensing this Indigenous, animistic, spiritual path.

You know, otherwise, if not for this kind of understanding, we are just controlled by consumerist society. Buy a house, buy a good car, have two children and send them to university – that's the only happiness people can conceive in this society.

They want you to think happiness has to do with material possession, rather than life.

And without another sense of existential happiness, it's like we're lost already. Even if socialism comes, you know. Like more people have cars, that's what socialism is about.

The problem is materialism. Use the metaphor of a coin. So there's a materialist coin: one side is capitalism, the other side is socialism. It's the same coin. It's all based on this material world, rather than the interaction with real, natural phenomena. It's all about the man-made. Like Marx was obsessed with the idea of the means of production. Who cares about the means of production? What's essential is the means of living! How do you live?

So one thing I wanted to ask: when you went into the wilderness, you were living in nature, with limited material...

I had no unnecessary material. I gave up everything. I gave up comfort. Do you know, I stayed wet for weeks at a time.

And cold right?

And cold! And hungry. And worried.

But you chose to do that, right? Behind your decision to do it, you had a different vision of what's important for your life.

That was the reason for doing it. I used to say, "I wanna go back to ground zero." To live with as little as possible, and see what is necessary.

And then, instead of commodity, I imagine you encountered a really rich world. Instead of the commodity object you were facing the living world, nature, universe. So it's not just a reduction – it's a new discovery of existence. You must

have achieved some kind of incredible happiness, within this hardship. Isn't that so?

I did. It was the happiest I'd ever been in my life, and maybe will ever be. To reach that point where you and this universe are connected. You're completely unprotected. Vulnerable. You're just like, "here I am."

Maybe it's the same vulnerability. Whether you're facing the State, or the forces of the universe...

Yes!

And you experienced that, it was just you and your wife, alone in the wilderness.

Right. If you make a wrong move you're dead! Nobody even knows you're there.

Yeah, nobody cares.

No! But that's the truth of reality! Nature doesn't care. The cosmos can send a disaster that can kill millions of people. You don't think the cosmos loses any sleep thinking "oh I killed a million people today."

In a sense your concept of struggle expanded, by going into the wilderness. It expanded beyond the immediate political context.

And it changed the daily struggle. It made the daily struggle have a larger goal. To survive to find another way, to build a new life.

One question I originally wanted to ask: among your comrades who left New York and went out west, was there anybody else who had this consciousness of the warrior?

Not exactly.

So do you think that the Pancho Villa syndrome comes from a lack of this awareness? Like sustaining the revolutionary impetus, but without some greater, spiritual perspective?

Yes. And a lot of those people, including myself, had been criminalized as youth. So after the militant struggle ended, it was easier to fall back into that.

To fall back into criminal groups, like gangs?

Yes.

Which can be revolutionary in this society, though.

Right. And after the revolution fails they go back. That was Pancho Villa. He was a bandit before the revolution, and after the revolution he returned to it.

Have you ever heard of Sri Aurobindo? He was a revolutionary in India. He was an armed revolutionary fighting against the British colonist. And eventually, he was imprisoned, and he became spiritual. He came out and he became like a guru, you know, he formed an ashram. He became a spiritual person. So it's interesting, because at some point he had seen that the violent revolutionary no longer had a purpose. But he didn't become a bandit. He went toward the spiritual understanding. And I always thought about him because in a sense, that's more parallel to me.

You experienced that yourself.

Right. I saw that the Pancho Villa path was a dead end. And I could see that this other path might lead somewhere, where you could still help people. So I went that way. My own brother went the Pancho Villa way. And he got shot.

Do you think that pushed you away from the Pancho Villa path?

No, I was already starting to go that way. And I tried to get him to go with me. Did I ever tell you the story about it? He was already hooked onto this Pancho Villa path. And I was moving this other way. And I always had this fantasy that maybe I could pull him with me. Pull him away from…I didn't know if that was possible, I had my doubts. But I thought it was worth it to try.

There used to be a cafe in New Mexico that, whenever I passed, I would stop to see if he was there. We used to hang out there, we would go there together. So we would look for each other there. And one time, my wife and I stopped to look for him, and he was there. So we sat together and drank coffee and visited. And I told him about this path I was pursuing. I said "I really want to share it with you. I want to take you with me, to see what you think. You make up your own mind."

At first he said no. He said "how can we give up who we were? We were somebody!" He actually used that term, "we were somebody." I told him "yes, we'd have to give up who we were. But who we were is over. It's done, you can't be who you were anymore. But this path you're going down is not…" So we argued. He was younger than me. He said to me, "you know brother, you're older than me. And I argue with you, but you know I always try to listen to you." He said, "I'll go with you. I'll look and see what I think." I said "that's all I want. You look for yourself." He said okay.

This was about a Tuesday or a Wednesday. Maybe Tuesday. And that weekend I was going to a ceremony. I said "this Saturday, I'm going to a ceremony." He said "okay, I'll go with you. I'm gonna find out." We shook hands, told each other how we were gonna meet, said okay and shook hands. We hugged. And I left.

That Thursday, he got killed. He got shot. He was gonna go with me Saturday. But he got killed on Thursday. So I never knew if he would join me on that path. I still don't know.

when the vast body moves thru battlefield streets
it walks on many legs
hungry cells and angry bellys
guts of anger/blood of anger
anger in the one fantastic throat that cries:
"Now.'Now this body sees, this body feels
this body knows and aches, this body
will suffer to be chained no more!"
and when the vast body moves thru battlefield streets
the great buildings tremble...

henry/uaw-mf

DAY SEVENTEEN

We've talked about the turning point when you decided to go to the mountains, as Reich said. But also in the Lower East Side, you were facing critical situations with people in crisis, for example taking care of runaways. Through doing that, do you think you changed yourself a lot too? Already then your practice was not just protest and fighting in the street.

The protest and fighting in the street was a small part. The other part was living! The activism was part of the living. The living wasn't part of the activism.

That's often confused in the political milieu.

It's confused amongst some political people because they want to control all movement. We didn't want to control anything. We just wanted to share with each other to build something together. There was no organization, no hierarchy. There wasn't that sense of direction and control.

And people always talk about democracy — it's a word that's often misused. It's not voting, that's bullshit. Democracy is that you're building together, you figure out how you're gonna do something.

And if you don't agree you work it out, "well how about this, how about…" I mean it's a living process.

We never voted. Not in the Lower East Side, or at the homestead. Not once. You just do what you're gonna do, and if somebody disagrees strongly, well, go do what you want. See you later, you know. There was no sense of control, like "this is what we want everyone to do."

You know in Marxism or religion, the idea of salvation or liberation tends to claim you have to help everybody. You have to make a world that's good for everybody. I'm increasingly doubtful about this. One cannot save everybody.

No! You can save the person next to you. Maybe.

Or "see you later" is the right attitude. Like white supremacist people, I don't want to save them. I just want to say goodbye, I don't want to see you again. This is essentially different from the universalist principle that wants to liberate everyone. Because there's no way of liberating these people, you know?

The problem is that it's based on an ideology, that is considered to be correct. And that idea of being correct means that everybody must understand what's correct. That's why political correctness is bullshit. One doesn't have to be politically correct. One has to be karmically correct.

Karmically correct?

In other words, correct in relation to the universe. Not correct in relation to people. In the universe, the concept of correctness has no bearing. The universe is not correct, or incorrect. It just is. And you have no choice! You can't change the universe. The universe can change you. But you cannot change the universe.

This brings me to what I was thinking about today: the problem with believing that you are controlling anything. Like say the pandemic, the coronavirus. This might sound weird, but the coronavirus, that entity is not man-made. It was provoked by human actions, but it's not man-made. It's part of creation. You cannot go to war with creation. You have to figure out what it is, and how to go around it. Because creation cannot be changed — it is the change. It is reality itself. You cannot change it. And there is no hierarchy. The coronavirus, once it exists, is as real as the human. The universe doesn't distinguish "oh, this is a human! That's more important than this little virus." Both exist. That's it. The Western mind doesn't understand that.

Like the other day, I heard this doctor being interviewed about the pandemic, talking about the vaccine. He said "we're making a vaccine so smart that it'll be able to deal with the virus that mutates." He's talking about how they're gonna fight this virus. He spoke for half an hour, and he never once talked about the origin of the virus. How we have destroyed the balance of nature, which allowed the virus to overcome our natural defense. He never said "we've got to go back and correct what we've done wrong." No, he's trying to figure out how we're gonna kill the virus. He said "we're gonna make vaccines smarter and smarter." But the virus is smarter than him! It mutates, as he speaks! Because it's organic, it's nature. It's not a product. It comes from creation. In a sense, we allowed it. Because we destroyed the organic protections against it.

And I thought to myself, that's what they did with antibiotics. They overused them to a degree where there are actually super bugs now. So what's gonna happen when they have a super virus? They keep finding ways to defeat the virus, well the virus is gonna outsmart them, and there will be a virus that there's nothing they can do. I don't know if that makes sense…

Yeah, like it's this whole history of only treating nature as a thing to dominate. There's no understanding of the interrelationality, and the consequences.

Because they think they're in control. Like this guy, I wish you could've seen him. You know, I believe a person's face, more than I believe a person's words. And the whole time, I was watching his face. His face was so egotistic. He really believed he was in control. He was like a general, organizing a war. He's at war with creation! Well, creation can make a virus that'll eat him for lunch!

But do you know, I have never heard a single person from the medical world say anything to the degree that they caused covid. This materialist, capitalist way of life caused it by the destruction of the natural world. They have never owned up to that. And yet they want to make it like "well now we have the vaccine." The whole import of what this guy was saying is look how brilliant we are that we came up with a vaccine. It's a slick PR job. They caused it! And yet they want to get this great honor of solving it.

I feel that the logic is reversed. They say Covid came to us, but we went to it. We made the world such that Covid could happen.

Not only that, but they eliminated — just take a simple thing like food. Most people think food is just something you eat. It's not. Food is essential to the balance of your body. Food is actually a medicine. And they poison the food! So you don't have that medicine anymore. So your immune system is weakened. Then they intrude in the animal world, and our immunity is already weakened…And they never talk about it! They never say that the way to correct the problem is to go back to having some balance in life that they destroyed. They want to continue doing what they've done. Just have a vaccine, and continue a life based on destruction.

The whole thing is just about keeping the economy going. This is sick, destroying the whole planet for the sake of the economy.

Rather than understanding nature, this culture wants to dominate it. That's why we have pandemics. That's why the world is toxic. That's why there's people eating food with no nutrition. How can you stay healthy with no nutrition? Food was health, originally. It's what nature put to sustain us, like there are certain foods that you eat that have certain vitamins, and fulfill different needs that your body has. Nature provided it! To give you sustenance. But they poisoned all of that. So you have toxicity. You have pandemics. And as long as the capitalist, materialist way of life is dominant, you're gonna continue to have pandemics, storms, hurricanes, all of that. They're gonna be worse. They're part of nature, but they're exacerbated. Now they're catastrophic. I don't know how to put it in scientific terminology, but if the climate is warmer, then the energies are more devastating. Like the storms become more intense.

In other words, there's a connection between what you do, and how nature responds. It's almost like saying if you mess with nature, nature is going to mess with you. They go together: if you misuse nature, it's going to come back, and bite you.

That's karma.

Exactly. But at one time, you know when they talk about paradise, at one time this was paradise. Everything fit. What we call disease today didn't exist because everything worked in harmony, the food had antibodies, everything you needed. But the minute you destroy a part, that gives ascendency to a part, which might be more malignant. Does that make sense?

Well, I don't precisely know where it starts, the destruction of harmony. I can't believe there was ever harmony. There was always sickness and death.

There was a harmony in the sense that everything was organic, and evolved organically. Like plants grew, and they benefitted people.

But it's natural that you can only live so long. I mean that *is* harmony, things die! There's nothing wrong with death.

In a sense I agree with you, because somehow the Western civilization considers eternal life. And humans are entitled to eternal life, and Western civilization should expand all over. Maybe this is the beginning of the destruction. You know how in Hollywood films sometimes God will appear played by some actor like Charlton Heston? It's disgusting! The presentation of God as a white man is so disgusting.

Yeah. God's got a beard, and he's sitting in a chair.

And always portrayed as an old man. It's so stupid.

See, that is one of the first things that has to be dealt with — the concept of an anthropomorphic god. There is *no* anthropomorphic god. That's why many Native cultures thought of it as a mystery. You cannot define it. It is defining you! You're not going to define it.

But there are certain things, even little things, that this culture doesn't understand. It's so simplistic that I'm almost embarrassed to mention it, but take a simple thing like sugar. They stuff our children full of sugar, right? Everything is advertised to draw children to sugar. And then they wonder why they have a crisis with addiction. They are creating addicts as children, they're getting them addicted to sugar. Then those kids grow up being addicts, and they wonder why. They don't think that their stupid purple and pink cereal leads to addiction. But it does! That's what karma means, like you do things correctly. And then you don't have a problem. But if you do things some stupid way, you're gonna end up with a problem!

Or if you make people think there's an anthropomorphic God. I use the word "god" in the small sense, like there's this white man with a beard, sitting in a chair. There isn't! There's creation. There's the universe. There's life. And you should be talking about that.

Instead you're teaching children there's some guy with a beard sitting in a chair — well there isn't! So that's not going to help them in their lives. If you told them, this whole universe is woven together, maybe that would help them. But instead your earliest teachings are completely wrong.

I really feel that. And then people pretend like death doesn't exist. I mean I was terrified as a child, I couldn't sleep at night thinking about dying, and no one ever talked to me about it. They don't tell kids about death!

That's something that children should grow up understanding. If there is life, there is death. It's impossible to have life without death. They go together! They're part of the same — it's one. Creation is one. They're not opposed, like one's positive, one's negative.

Maybe this approaches a subject you can't discuss so much. I mean the pursuit of spirituality, and your personal beliefs.

Yes and no. I'll talk about it in terms of animism. Animism is a broader understanding of the universe. It's saying the whole thing is connected. The universe is connected. Like what exists in the universe, exists in us. There's a whole universe in each of us. Nobody talks about it. You're a walking universe!

Or like how people talk about being anti-war. They don't ever talk about the fact that your body is at war. The antibodies are fighting diseases, the viruses are being attacked. You want to kill them. That's pro-war!

I would even say sometimes killing, you know? Killing should also be affirmed. We cannot negate wolves eating deer. We can't tell the wolves, "you shouldn't kill deer."

No! Because that's part of creation. That's nature. I mean it's built on that. Smaller life-forms are eaten by bigger life-forms, that are eaten by bigger and bigger life-forms. And microscopic life-forms eat them all. Life is self-perpetuating. It feeds on itself.

And some people want to stop killing animals. But have you ever heard anyone say, "well what about plants?" Why doesn't anybody ever talk about that? What about grass? Maybe grass got a mother and father. And you're pulling it out without even thinking!

So for you animism isn't just being respectful of some idea of wholesome nature. It's also killing, war...You have to interact in the full sense.

You are part of this whole process. And your part is not to control the other parts. Your part is to coexist, to understand it and be part of it. This whole thing is in motion!

Within the human world, what kind of killing is affirmed is a difficult question. But I like to think about it, you know?

Yeah. All these things have to be thought through. They're philosophical. It's not that we should all come to the same conclusion. It's that we have to think about it. We must be aware.

Like there's a movement now against guns. I mean it's obvious that something's wrong, all these people are out there with guns and ammunition, killing people for no reason. It's obvious that there's a problem. So some liberals want to ban guns. But if you ban guns, what does that mean then? Only the military and the police have guns? Disarm all the young people in the ghetto, so that only the police have weapons? How do you defend yourself, if only the authority has guns?

That's an important, tough question.

And you know, there are serious problems. I don't know what the solutions are. But it's like nobody understands these things. Nobody tries to go beyond the surface. That's what I've been doing for eighty years: don't dismiss something as positive or negative. Try to keep looking at it, to see below the surface. But this society has done the opposite. So we're stuck. It's like this guy making vaccines. And by making vaccines, he's allowing the original problem to remain.

So more pandemics will follow.

They never try to solve what caused it, because they think they solved the problem.

It's not a solution, it's a postponement.

But they think it's a solution. So they don't deal with the real problem: to reverse what they're doing wrong. But in all honesty, I don't have enough time left to try to explain these things. If I had another eighty years, it still wouldn't be enough time. This culture lost animism. It took hundreds and hundreds of years to lose it. So it's going to take many years to re-engage it.

Indigenous people didn't necessarily understand it — they lived it. So they found different solutions. Some of the solutions we may not agree with. Some we may even consider odious. But they all found some way to solve the problem of how to live in the universe. Through living, they reached different understandings. And now those understandings are all being lost.

I remember as a youngster how Apache people were feared. They would bury enemies in the ground and let ants eat them alive. And people were like "oh my god, stay away from those Apaches!" Well, the Apaches were a small band of people, and they created such fear that nobody wanted to mess with them. And they survived.

We don't know how or why these solutions came about. We just have to understand that life has its own way.

That's a beautiful way to put it. Instead of just people, life is the animating agent.

And it's like, thousands of years of life. We talked about that one man in the Amazon, that was the last of his tribe. He was the last person who could speak their language, the last person who knew the ways they had. It took thousands of years for his people to bring this consciousness to him. It was passed down to him, and then it ended with him. That's it! It's over. People don't realize how important that is. It happens every day. Across the planet, languages are dying. And within each language is a way of thinking that will never be expressed again. Whatever those people understood about life, about plants, about the Earth...You cannot recreate it.

Do you think these languages, with these different worldviews, also allowed for different ways of being and relating?

Right. And they were important to see the multiplicity. They all found different ways to be, ways to live, ways to understand. And it would have helped to see all these different multiple conclusions. But so many of them have been lost, and the remaining dominant ones are like one-dimensional. They caused the problem. They exterminated the others. So now we're stuck with that loss.

I think it's even built into the grammar, in the way these languages evolved. Imperial languages are more transactional and easy to abstract, while Indigenous languages are more relational, and connected to place.

And they might have had something that was closer and more correct, but we won't know. It's like what happened was that the worst destructive force was able to destroy those forces that could have helped.

Yeah, with guns and capitalism and religion, European nations colonized the world. And really their impetus was to exploit the land.

They're trying to turn the world into a commodity. They're still doing it. Western culture is a mistake. When the colonizer came to this continent, they could have learned from the people that were here. Native people could have helped them. They would've said, "you guys are really messed up. Let us show you." They could have! But instead the colonizer tried to force them to follow the mistake. Rather than learning from their ways, they wanted to make them part of the mistake. It's backwards! They should have done the opposite. They should have gone to the Indigenous and said, "help us change our ways."

And since then, everything they've done has been backwards.

But Ben, I think something you're saying that is so important, is that there's the universe, we have to relate to life in the universe, but there's also the universe inside. That's where these spiritual practices come in, like your description of medicine, I mean people need something like that. Because actually there's a lot of terror in experience, in the universe inside, you know?

The universe inside is at constant war! Then you got people walking around with signs saying "no more war." Their bodies are at war as they're walking around with the sign! The reason they are alive is because the body is at war, killing off the germs.

So it's a real disconnect with the inside.

The problem is that the inside and the outside are not separate. They are one. That's animism. It's all one. What's in you, and what's out here, are one. There's no distinction.

In other words, the universe is connected. It's alive. There's a spiritual entity throughout the universe — it's not only a material existence, the spirit of life is dominant. All of life is based on motion, this spirit, this movement throughout the universe.

There is no end to life. Life is an energy; when you pass, it changes form. So you are given life somehow, but life is not "yours." It's a gift, so to speak, that you have to return.

In the spiritual domain, I think Buddhism and a lot of Native cultures, as I understand, paid respect to death.

Absolutely. You have to!

But capitalism is totally ignoring the importance of death. It tries to live forever, through the expansion of wealth. That, to me, is the source of the problem.

That is a problem. It's an inability to face reality. The reality is that death is part of life. It's not just a verbal metaphor, it's real. There is no life without death. And this culture lost the ability to understand that.

But you know, I feel that within some cultures, like in Japanese culture, there's still an understanding of the role that death plays. I think they have it more than Western culture. Western culture has no ancestor worship, no recognition of those that came before us, and passed it on to us. They don't talk about what went before them. I think Indigenous people always recognize that, the importance of their ancestors. And some cultures still have remnants of that mentality. But some cultures totally forgot it.

Then the question is: how to recover animism? If these animistic ways are all being lost, and it took thousands of years to develop them...

I don't think we have that much time. So we have to look at the ways that are still here, and try to learn from that understanding that you are part of nature. And find ways to replicate that attachment.

Another thing I wanted to ask, in relation to your community:

how do people approach mortality, illness, aging...How do you deal with death?

You don't have to deal with death. Death is a constant. It's just there. If something is alive, it faces death. There is no life without death. So that idea that death is a negative, is a mistake. It's just a result of living. You could speed it up, or you could slow it down. But ultimately you have to accept death. It's not up to us, what lives and what dies.

And you try to learn from the mistakes. Maybe some deaths were caused by accidents, or by inappropriate activities. So you have to learn from it. If you caused the death, then you have to correct that causation. Like a lot of diseases that are rampant on Earth right now are human caused. Like cancer. Maybe there would be cancer independent of our mistakes, I can't say. But the fact of our mistakes has made cancer a scourge. We made it balloon, by our mistakes. We've done everything wrong.

But my question is in your community, how do people deal with death, within themselves? Like rituals, communal understandings...

I understand. It's important that people find a way to ceremonialize both life and death. I can't say how others should do it. Everybody must find a way. I can't tell other people how to do what I did, because they may not have the same belief I have.

So if I talk about myself: my family belongs to a temple in Japan, the family grave is there. But this temple is based on monetized exchange, you know, the monks drive Mercedes-Benz'. I don't want to be part of this filthy institution with these capitalist monks. I don't want to go there when I die. I want to face my death somehow in a different way. But I don't know how because I don't have a spiritual tradition. This kind of thing I want to ask you, because it's important for

everybody. Many people have no tradition they can connect with on a spiritual level.

Right. But that's the question. You have to find a way. What feels right, you have to seek it out.

I see. So everybody has to find it on their own.

Yeah. Or find others to share it with. And I agree with you, that that is a big vacuum. I don't know what the solution is, in general. Only as an individual. I found my solution. But if you just sit and say "well I don't have anything," you'll never have anything. So you have to say, "I better start looking."

Anyway, you got a lot today.

Today was a big day. Today is very important to me. It's a new dimension of statement coming from you.

To be honest, it's a dimension that I never really talked about. I don't know how to transmit it. That's why I removed myself.

But I'm glad I asked you this question, because it's really my own problem. To me it's so important that I refuse this temple. It's a serious issue for me. I'm always curious why politically radical friends of mine don't have the same question. After they die, where are they gonna go? Throw their ashes into the ocean, or what, don't they imagine? Do they imagine they're gonna die in a hospital bed? In a field? Isn't that important to think about, as part of a political practice? I'm curious why people don't talk about this as a serious issue.

Because they're afraid of it. But we have to feel secure in the fact that wherever we go, it's a good place. Whether we know it or not. See…it's the only place. So it has to be good. You have no choice, they don't come to you and say "do you wanna go there, or do you wanna go elsewhere?" No, you go where they send you.

And in reality, the only people concerned about where you go when you die, or what happens when you die, are living people. Dying people don't have to think about it. The moment you have a thought, it's gone. So you only have so long to have that thought. At some point, you go back. You pass on, you become…You float around for a while.

Or like some people, like certain Buddhists say "you're gonna come back in another life." So you might come back as a worm. And that became a threat, "if you keep doing that, you're gonna come back as a worm!" But a worm's alright.

And in any case, what you just said, that's really important. That it's all the same place. So it has to be good. For me that is really helpful.

You should be assured, you have no choice. There's no line here or there, you have to choose.

Good. I can quit worrying about that at least.

You can rest assured.

KNOW YOURSELF
KNOW YOUR PEOPLE

ARMED LOVE

MOTHERFUCKERS

DAY EIGHTEEN

I feel there is something important we are hearing from your struggles to build community. Because many of our comrades tend to be together as only one generation. But in your case, you had elders, now you are an elder, you adopted many children – you had a multi-generational community. This is very important to learn.

It's very important. But you have to create it. In other words, it won't fall into your lap. You have to consciously realize how important it is. Like we talked about that book by Wilhelm Reich, *The Murder of Christ*. For me, it was like Reich said: rather than staying and being a martyr in Jerusalem, Christ should have gone to the mountains, to work amongst the people. So that was part of it, I had that thought in my mind.

So that thought helped you to consciously shift the focus of struggle. But it seems that there were parallels, or some continuation from your struggles in the Lower East Side, no?

Well, in a sense, I started adopting kids back then. Not in the full sense. But I realized the need. For instance I had friends, a man and a woman, and they had a baby. They were drug addicts. And the man got sentenced, he'd been arrested and he was sentenced to jail. So the woman was raising the child by herself. And one day I was out on the street and someone ran over and told me that this woman had been arrested. I asked, "what about the baby?" They said they didn't know. So I went to their apartment and the baby was there, alone. So I took her. I got a backpack, a kind of baby carrier, and I used to wear the baby on my back. I took care of her. But I was an activist, you know, I was always in danger. So at some point I realized that it was untenable to carry this baby around. And there was a couple that wanted to take her, a New Age couple that lived part time in New York and part time in a commune, I think it was in Vermont. I was reluctant to give up the child, I really didn't want to do that. But I felt like I had to, for the child's sake.

And then, sometime later, I found a boy. He might've been about 12, or maybe even 14. I found him sleeping in the hallway of one of our buildings where we had a crash pad. So I invited him in. We kind of adopted him then, he was always with us. It wasn't that he just stayed in the crash pads. He became like a family member.

So that fit the concept that Reich had, that you should go out and help people, not be a martyr. Then when I went out west and we had a homestead, we had all this land, and a subsistence farm, so we started taking in kids. We took kids that were threatened, like their parents were alcoholics, or they had dysfunctional families. One boy we adopted as a newborn, we took him home from the hospital. Another we took when he was about 6 or 7 and we raised him until he was in his twenties. Some kids we had only a few years, some for less than a year — it depended on the situation. We had some kids that would come for the summer, and then sometimes they would stay on. So it would vary, depending on the time of year. Sometimes it would be only three or four kids. Sometimes in the summer we'd have from ten to twenty kids.

You lived there also with two other couples, you said?

Correct. There were two other families that shared the land with us. We each had our own home, we weren't a commune. We never felt comfortable with the idea of all living in the same household. We didn't believe that was a desired factor. Quite the opposite, we thought it was important that each family occupied their own world. But we lived on the same land and shared everything, the farm, the gardening, the lumber work. The three men worked as timber cutters, we did contracts together. The women did gardening, and they made crafts together. We did everything together. So you could say it was a communal effort — rather than a commune.

In today's sense it kind of sounds like a commune. But you preferred the word "homestead?"

To me, commune means that everyone lives together, in the same home. That's my understanding. So what we did was communal, in a sense. We worked together, and we were a community. But not a commune.

And you were sharing so much fundamental material, so as far as money goes it didn't matter so much that everyone had the same bank account or something.

No because we worked together, we were drawing similar salaries. I mean there was no separation. It wasn't dictated, it was just what we did.

You also grew your own food?

Yeah we had a large garden, maybe half an acre. And I used to hunt, and we had livestock. So we raised our own food. We didn't shop except for some staples. Like we would go every fall at harvest time and work at different farms, we'd harvest bushels of potatoes, and onions and carrots and things like that, and we'd store them in the root cellar. We'd fill the root cellar so we'd have them all winter.

And we always had one or two deer hanging in there, we had lots of meat, and eggs, we had chickens and hogs, you know, we were self-sufficient. We fed ourselves.

That's amazing.

That's what people should be doing! Because when this system collapses, how are you gonna eat? If you're dependent on this system for food, then when it collapses, you're out! So I encourage people to learn how to grow things, learn how to hunt, to be more self-sufficient.

We have friends in different parts of the world that are starting to do that. Like in Japan, in the mountains, we have a close group of friends. They're trying to do something like you did when you were homesteading. When this book is finished we'd like to translate it and show them, because they want to learn from your experience. They were impressed by the story of how you adopted children.

It's essential. It is political, in the real sense. People think politics is some abstracted relationship to power and structure. No! If you see children as essential to the future, and you try to share with them…

When you were homesteading, you started growing food, you discovered different uses of plants, you were making crafts — all these things you developed yourself? Or you learned from Native people there?

Yeah from the local population, Mexican, Native American. And from reading, and from other people too. I mean there are a lot of counterculture people who know about herbs, you know, it's not unknown amongst the counterculture. There's some understanding of the balance, the need. So there was that, there were Mexican people who had been living on the land, there were Native people, there were books — you need it all. And you piece it together. It's like a quilt, you put the pieces together.

Also it's helpful how you described this idea of medicine, that there's so many ways that could be medicine.

That I really learned from Native people. To them "medicine" is a key word. Everything's a medicine. How you do things, what you eat, how you think, it's all a medicine. I've never encountered another culture having that consciousness. I think we talked about this way of life where you never turn yourself around: that's a medicine! They have an understanding of medicine that's not just about medical treatment.

It's not an object, it's more a way of being in the universe.

Exactly. Your whole way of life is built on it. It's not like you live some distracted way of life, and take a pill. It's the opposite. Your life is the pill.

I was thinking after our last discussion, about how this homogeneous capitalist civilization is eating up all these different ways of life, different languages and cultures. I wanted to ask your sense, based on your personal experience of trying to create new community, do you have a sense of if it would it be possible to create something different from this?

It's very possible. But it's a long process and you have to find a method. I was thinking about it yesterday, I'm glad you brought it up. I was going through the internet and there was an article about these towns that are the poorest in America. The median income is like 10,000 dollars a year. And I was thinking, what if young people went to these places — because now people are on the internet, they could make a living — they could go and create an alternative society, in a town that's dying. I mean people could survive, and build alternative communities, instead of being in cities like New York. Different groups could go to different areas.

Some people we know are doing something like that. But then the problem, say there's a handful of people who go, and then they start fighting, and within two years their relations break down. So the struggle is really internal as well as external, like you were saying. But there's not much focus on that.

And it seems the preponderance of thought leans toward how to get rid of what exists, with very little thought about what to replace it with. And I think we need more people thinking about that. I was at a gathering one time and a Native American activist said, I thought it was really interesting the way she put it, she said, "you guys want this system to collapse. But you don't know how to grow food. You don't know how to hunt. You don't know how to make things, or repair things. So then what do you do when this system collapses?"

In other words, it seems to me that people have to focus as much on what to build, as on what needs to be destroyed. Like it's easy to say "get rid of capitalism." That's easy, it's a slogan! But what are you going to replace it with? Centralized authoritarian Stalinism? And that's why at times you end up with that. Because nobody's thinking about what to create, they're mostly thinking about what to destroy. But we have to start thinking of what we are going to build.

We know what we have to destroy, but do we know how to replace it? What would an alternative look like? Some people in the '70s tried communes, that wasn't it. That wasn't enough. And nobody has ventured past that yet.

Will you say more about why communes didn't work?

While I never lived in a commune, I visited a lot of them. And instinctually I felt that their goal wasn't workable. Like the idea that everyone in the commune is of one mind. And the impulse to create sameness is the wrong energy.

If you look at some tribal societies, the idea isn't that we're all sharing equally. The idea is that we're all living together, sharing, but we're still individuals. They had some balance where they were tribal *and* they were individual. You have to share, and be together, but you can't give up your individuality. Everybody contributed what they were able to individually, but it wasn't because they were all equal. The word "equal" is confusing. They had some understanding of the balance between the individual and the group.

So I think this time around, people have to build communities, but remain individuals within the community. The idea of the commune just didn't work. We don't need sameness. We all have different abilities, different needs. And we have to find a way to work together. In a sense, the word "mutual" is better. We're all working together, and sharing together. But we don't give up our individuality.

I think part of the problem is confusing individuality with individualism. You're talking about individuality in terms of lived existence. It's not just abstract, like "individualism is bad." It's a mode of existing in the universe, the individual being.

Right. And the concept of the tribe was more real. In the tribe everybody is an individual person, but they have unity as a people. Things happen organically. Like say the tribe is hunting. Well there are certain people who are more proficient at hunting, so they become recognized as skilled hunters. There's nothing wrong with that, you want somebody who is a better hunter. They can help organize the hunt. They can say "well this is a better day, this is a better way to go." Whereas somebody else may have no idea. So why not rely on the person who knows? But the communal impulse was to say "no, we have to be equal." And I think that's a mistake, to repress individuality and create a homogenized being. People who are strong individuals are gonna resist it and leave. Like "I'm not the same as this person, this guy's an idiot!"

I don't know how to put it in words, but you could just feel it. People should not have to hide their ability, so that everybody feels comfortable. That ability should be utilized, not discouraged or discarded. You want skilled people to be part of your community. Your tribe. Your group. So that was the downfall of communes, that effort to force everybody to be the same. The effort should be to cooperate and build together, and let different skills be appreciated.

It's like the commune's ideal was based on a sense of what would make the individual feel good, rather than what would be best for the community.

And people are afraid of creating a hierarchy. But there's nothing wrong with difference. Say one person is good at hunting, well another person may be good at butchering, or gathering plants — no skill is lesser. That whole way of thinking itself has to change, that any one activity is superior, or more socially valuable than another.

Life is organic. You don't have to plot everything out, some things make sense. It's okay to be different. And to rely on self-regulation, and inclination. The key is mutuality. It's not that everybody has to be the same, but everybody has to come together.

It reminds me of the poster you showed us, "know yourself, know your people." I think that gets to the heart of the problem: who are your people, and how do you understand your relation to them? It's really a vital question. And really tricky, especially for people who aren't Indigenous.

Yeah, it's like the chasm between the individual and the people is really deep, and hard to cross. It's hard to understand.

That's the question that's always difficult with Japan. Revolution wouldn't happen in Japan, I believe, so long as people think they're Japanese.

Well, yeah. As long as you think you're any nationality, and you don't understand the wider perspective, whatever you do is going to be limited. I mean, you can't change life, if you're coming at it from a national perspective.

And especially in Japan, because there's no outside in society. Of course non-Japanese exist. But the society is too much unified in a scary way. So one thing we have to do in Japan is to decompose the nation-state society.

You can't eliminate being Japanese. We're born, we are what we are. But you can eliminate the concept that you belong to some special group. You know, I've never really talked to you about this, but I'd be curious about the Ainu. Like how do they fit in to Japanese consciousness.

They are Indigenous inhabitants of the archipelago, who over a long period of time were gradually pushed more and more north by Japanese forces. Then in the late-19th century Japan invaded their territories in what's now called Hokkaido, and they were deprived of land and culture and assimilated. But still there are small groups, small villages exist, and they try to preserve their culture.

Do they still have a spiritual tradition?

I think small groups of people are still doing it. I don't think it's as strong as many Native American traditions. But they try to relearn, and there's a hunting ritual — they were a hunting culture — and their singing as a way of communicating with nature, that kind of tradition exists.

So that would be important to enter the Japanese consciousness, probably. Just like America cannot go forward without understanding Native people that were here. They can't do it.

And in America there are still many substantial Native groups and territories. So do you think that non-Native people should learn from Native people, like young people should go and build relationships and try to learn from their traditions?

Well I think they are, to a degree. And my hope is that more and more people will see that there was a way of life here before European domination, and look to it and try to understand...Like in the '60s, when I started using Native designs, I felt that the Native consciousness was not just national, or racial. There was something in the air, there was something here that I could absorb and become closer to — that was my hope. And so, when I went out west, I felt like here's my chance to try to understand what Native people understood. And in that is the understanding of animism.

But unfortunately, as some people are moving toward Native, animistic understanding and absorbing some of that, Native people are moving more and more toward accepting the materialist, capitalist world, and losing their own understanding. They're both happening at the same time. But one thing I've always felt is that, it's not important that you see the outcome of your effort. The outcome is out of your control. What's important is that you make the effort. You can't say "well that's not gonna happen, so why bother?" You have to do what you can to bring about the outcome you believe in, regardless, and then see if it happens. Because nobody alive would make an effort if they thought it was already futile. Everybody strives toward some goal. Say like Palestinians, they don't say "well we just have to accept the fact that we're colonized, and that we're under apartheid" — they have to resist. You have to resist, without thinking of which way...

It's incredible to think of the power of this capitalism and settler colonialism, attacking and expanding, and yet Native people resisted for so many years, their territory, their culture. That's so important. They're still resisting. So we have to learn from them.

I think so. Personally, that was my approach.

Yeah, that's what you were doing. You did it.

And I agree with you one hundred percent that that's our hope. That's how I got involved with this animistic ceremonial world. It's an alternative to the dominant culture, which is not only harmful to the universe — it eliminates our humanity. Every oppressive system has to have people who are victims, that are willing to go along with the victimizer. The victimizer cannot be successful alone. Like in order for capitalists to succeed, they have to get a majority of people who are not capitalists to go along with them. So it's a constant effort to try to keep as many people as possible from falling into the dominant culture. And the move toward Indigenous ways of thinking and being is a help. Not everybody will make a total break. Maybe some people make a little break, and then some make a bigger break, and just a few make a total break. But you want everybody to move in that direction, to weaken the dominant culture.

It reminds me of your idea of relativity.

You have to encourage a break, even if it's partial. Both to strengthen the resistance, but also to weaken the dominant. It's parallel. Most people don't think about it. But I think that's important to recognize, that the building of a counter-resistance is parallel to the weakening of the dominant.

I like the relativity of the revolutionary animism that you're talking about—to me that's really hopeful. Because we can't just create new cultures. So from one perspective it feels impossible, if Indigenous cultures are going to be lost more and more. But what you're saying is more hopeful, because it's relative. You can move toward another way of being, even if you can't create a whole alternative culture.

Right. In other words, like I always say, revolution is not an event. It's a way of life. So you're not looking for an end — you're looking for the process to move toward that end. And it might take generations.

But my hope is that more and more people will become conscious of that Indigenous, animistic understanding and belief. And I think the fact that more and more non-Indigenous people are attracted to Indigenous ways and spiritual understandings — I think that's a positive. And I think it's stronger than most people realize. More and more people are trying to connect to Native ceremonial ways, both North American and South American. It's a big movement, I mean, I don't think people realize. Like I was trying to move toward it in the '60s. You could see it was there, but very slightly. And I pushed totally into it. But it's really growing, it's everywhere. It's not publicized, but there's a lot of people involved. I mean a lot.

That's very inspiring.

Yeah! And I'm totally involved, because there's so many people everywhere. It's becoming more and more dominant. And the relativity angle: even if some people don't go totally into it, it's still important to understand that there's something other than this materialist, money-oriented world. There's something. Even if they don't go completely to it, at least their recognition that there's something can help. I think that's really a bright spot, that it's becoming possible for more and more people to understand that animistic possibility.

Another hopeful tendency, which I think is complementary, are all these people making efforts to reconnect with nature and live more off of the land. Like our friends in the Pacific Northwest, they're learning about wetland ecology and trying to restore the wetlands, and cultivating plants, and building infrastructure for communal life. There's so many little groups like that finding different ways to connect with the Earth, in different environments.

That's very important. There's people doing that all over. Like I know people in Colorado and New Mexico doing that, trying to learn what it means to live on the land, trying to learn what it means to live together. And some political people might criticize it and say "well that's just self-interest." But my hope and my belief is that those groups at some point will find a way to connect. And that will become the basis of a new consciousness. Like all these groups in America, or like you said the group in Japan, all these different groups will find a way to communicate.

That's a hopeful image. Because alone what they're facing is so overwhelming. Basically every aspect of existence needs to be addressed. But it's encouraging to think that eventually these efforts can come together.

Yeah, and it will happen organically, you know. People are gonna find a way to connect and share. But the crucial thing is like you say, that they're doing what they're doing. The first stage is that people start to do what's necessary. That's more important than everybody meeting. It's more important that people do what they have to do. It's important that they start. You can't say, "well I don't wanna go off and do it alone." Because then it would never get done.

It goes back to the question: when this thing collapses, how are we going to survive? The people who are doing what you're talking about, they're gonna learn how to grow food, they're gonna learn how to make things, they're gonna learn about plants and medicines. They'll learn skills that could help when this thing collapses. They'll be able to make a counter-society. They'll survive. And they'll be more apt to push this thing's collapse, because they have an alternative. If you don't have an alternative, you know, do you really want it to collapse? So it's crucial.

And there's no time to waste. I mean, this thing is disintegrating fast. Faster than you can speak! We're at ground zero. The time is now.

ONE TIME A PEOPLE
EXISTED IN TOUCH
WITH THE EARTH
THEY WERE SMOTHERED
BY A DARKER FORCE
STRONGER THAN THEIR OWN
AND DRIVEN OFF THEIR LAND
THE SPIRIT OF THE LIGHTER
FORCES WENT INTO HIDING
AWAITING REBIRTH
NOW THE RAINBOW HAS REAPPEARED
GATHERING ITS PEOPLE
DRIVING THE DARKNESS INTO THE SEA
ARMED LOVE
MOTHERFUCKERS

DAY NINETEEN

When you were homesteading, already you had this consciousness that you experienced intense struggle in the city, and now you're doing something else. Were there other people like that in your community? Like people that came from the militant struggle, that shared the same kind of experience with you?

Well, I fell out of touch with most people. And in a lot of ways, the people that came from New York, I ended up being less connected to. Because they never grasped all the changes that I thought were necessary. They wanted to remain who they were. I didn't.

Like the heroic revolutionary?

Right. That was the Pancho Villa syndrome. I mean literally, when I talked to my kid brother about it, when I tried to get him to join me, he said "but how can we…we were somebody!" I told him "sure but who we were, that somebody is over. That somebody cannot survive. We have to find a new way to be."

Because you realized that that somebody was endangered.

And that somebody was not able to move into a new area where it was possible to continue to live. That somebody was going to clash with the powers. And I could see that we needed something additional to survive.

So it was really about survival. You had to find a way to survive in the new situation.

It's not only survival, it's reinvention. I felt that we had to reinvent ourselves. We were ready to confront the powers that be. But at some point, it became obvious that we weren't strong enough yet. There had to be a new consciousness, and people had to absorb and change the focus. It wasn't enough, the political struggle. We had believed that it was. But I could see that it wasn't. It needed a larger struggle.

And those people that didn't see that, if you continue that same confrontational struggle, there's no way you can survive. The powers that be had gained the upper hand. So you could continue to fight them in the same way, but it was suicidal. And I give them credit, those that try. If somebody wants to do that, I wouldn't deny them or say they were wrong. But I want to make it clear that, if you want to find a way to change it, to confront it, it's going to take time, and you'll have to have different understandings. You cannot just continue that one confrontational approach. Rather than running into the wall, you have to figure out how to dig under it and come up on the other side.

But you know, most people coming from the struggle couldn't do that. So there were those who continued the struggle, and couldn't survive. Then there were those who survived, that gave the struggle up. There were very few that said, "we're gonna continue the struggle, but on a different level." Which is what I wanted.

For me, adopting kids was part of the struggle. I don't know how to put it in words, but to me that was a necessity. It's like Reich had said, "don't go to Jerusalem, don't take the martyr's road." Find another way. And so, adopting and being involved with kids was part of that other way. The militarized approach had to be expanded.

You can't just focus on that.

Right. But you don't want to give up the struggle. I would never suggest people just accept the system as it is and stay safe. No. I'm against that. I don't want to accept the system. But I want to find another way to fight it. A way that we can continue the fight.

That's the reason to create a new kind of community, outside the dominant society.

And it's going to take time. Ten years, a hundred years? I don't know. It doesn't matter how long it takes.

It's like your sense of the struggle expanded, you saw it from a longer view?

It's almost like you expand the earthly struggle, and accept the struggle on a cosmic level. It's not just your daily life. It's a larger… more all-inclusive…

It's like giving up this modern politics. Or trying to go beyond it.

You have to! It's ironic because see, in the beginning, art was my focus. But at some point I realized that art was not enough. I had to add some political consciousness to it. So then that was the next phase, Black Mask, Up Against the Wall — added to the art. And it became social and political as well as art. But at some point I had to understand that *that* wasn't enough. Art, political, social, that wasn't enough. There's another dimension. And I recognized that. That need.

But in all honesty, I think that most people can only go so far. They reach a point where their growth process stops. It's really difficult for a person to say that what they're doing isn't sufficient. Most people can't do that, or won't do that. Say political people, if you try to talk to them about going past that struggle: they treat you as either a betrayer, or a fool. But I actually had to put the activist struggle on hold, in a sense, in order to find the path that could lead me to deeper change. That meant not focusing on the political struggle for a while, in terms of daily activity. But I didn't eliminate that part of my consciousness. I always felt that the world has to change. And I have to find a way to help change it.

In a sense urban struggle, or oppositional politics in the city is one thing. But the place you went, you were living with people who had a different spatiotemporality of struggle, over a longer history, right?

Yes. So I wanted to learn from them. I didn't want to bring to them who *I* was. I wanted to learn from them so that I could become something more. So I didn't want to tell them about what I had been doing.

You didn't tell them what you were doing in New York?

No.

Really! Not even in a small way, like personal background?

Well, you might meet somebody that you could share it with. But I didn't share it publicly.

But do you think you could have?

Theoretically, you could. But my personal feeling was that, by trying it, I would put myself at a distance from them that I didn't want to do. It would make me different. I wanted to go as a child. Not as an adult. Like when my brother said "but we were somebody" — I didn't want to be only that somebody.

You wanted to be nobody.

Not exactly. I wanted to go as a child. That's just me, I'm not saying everybody should do that. But that was my approach.

I can imagine how difficult, or impossible it would be to convince someone else. Like the others from your family, you couldn't convince them.

They could not do that, so they stayed...and a lot of them got killed. That's the Pancho Villa syndrome. It's hard to put it in words.

In other words, it's not that you give up the struggle. There were people who gave up the struggle, and became teachers, lawyers, you know, they became members of society. But my approach was that, I didn't give up the struggle, but I put the struggle in another dimension. I didn't articulate it, and express it as my ideology.

You just did it.

And I kept it in the back of my mind. I felt like, I'm going to learn what I have to learn from these people, as a child. I'm not going to forget what I already know. In the future I'm going to use it. And meld the two. Which, I feel like I did.

It's like you gained another life. You started another life.

So I'm neither. I'm neither that child anymore, nor am I the person that came out of the street struggle. I'm a whole new person.

You experienced two very distinct phases.

Well, way more than two! In other words, at one point I was an artist. At one point I was almost purely political. Then I went to the wilderness and that was another complete change. Then I went to the Native ceremonial world, and that was another complete change. That's where the spiritual part entered the combination of art, politics and spirituality. That's where that element came from.

This is a side comment, but I'm very impressed, and I feel that this is an important thing about you as an artist, that you don't try to use art as representing politics. You don't represent a political idea in your painting. Your painting is more existential.

You know, that's really important. I actually stopped painting for twenty years. I didn't give up being an artist, I remained an artist in my love of creativity and expression. But I stopped painting for twenty years. Because I couldn't do what I needed, I couldn't learn this new world if I remained a painter, as a physical artist.

Because of the time and energy...?

Because of the way of life that's needed. You need to dedicate time to it. Life became my art, in a sense. The physicality of it replaced painting. But I had to believe, when I stopped painting for twenty years, I had to feel and understand that I wasn't giving it up. It just was no longer the physical act. It was like activism. I stopped being an activist. But I didn't give it up mentally. I thought to myself, someday I'll do it again. Maybe someday I'll take a gun. But for the moment, it's not...It's hard to explain.

It's like a faith, that you could leave it and not lose it.

You have to believe in yourself. That you're not giving up. I mean literally, I quit painting for twenty years, and never felt like I gave up.

It's like you're going forward, but you're not clinging to the self. Or the relation to the self is more flexible. It's not "we were somebody" or "I'm an artist." It's more open. You didn't cling to the identity.

The safety of that identity, no.

But you were saying, for most people growth becomes less and less possible? How do you understand that? It's socially conditioned?

Partially. It's the nature of the human. You become accustomed to being a certain way. And age has something to do with it. Let's say you're a certain way for forty or fifty years. Then you quit changing, because who you are is set in your mind. I'm this person for forty or fifty years, that's it. It's very rare that a person says, "I'm willing to go and become a different person. To keep moving, to keep learning."

Think about it, I'm 80 years old. And I still try to keep going. I have no pension, no income. I'm still going! And at the age of eighty. Like, I'm an artist, right? But I detest the art world. I'm at odds with the art world. It's like my goal as an artist is to not be part of the art world. That's a tough place, when you think about it. And that's how I am with the political world. I'm active politically, but I detest political ideology. So I can't hang out with most political people.

And then in the spiritual world, you're a baby.

But now here's the problem: I grew up, right? But the people that I learned from, that I grew up with, they passed. And there's a new crop now, that don't know what those people said and what they did. And so I'm a little alienated from the people that followed, because the people I was involved with, they all passed.

It seems that the world is conspiring against you in a way.

Or I'm conspiring against it! So I'm totally alienated. I'm an artist that detests the art world. I'm a politically conscious person that dislikes most political people. And I'm a ceremonial person that feels that many people don't understand, they don't care about what's real anymore. Because they don't understand the way it was to begin with.

That means, in other words, to not be able to act in that transmitting position, is a real loss for you.

Right, that I can't honor those people that showed me, and continue to show other people what they did, or mention to other people what they thought. As these older people were passing, they said to me, "Ben don't forget what we did. Don't change it. Remember what we did." Well here's these young people changing it, but the dying words of these older people were "don't change it." So I'm more alienated from that world in a sense too now. I'm like an orphan.

That's the condition for Indigenous cultures everywhere today, I guess.

Yeah. But there are some young people who hear me, and they're interested in it. And they still want me around, to try to...But it's limited. But at least some of these ways can continue.

But then, for so many of us, the spiritual world has already disappeared. Friends move out to the country seeking a new way of life, but they don't have the spiritual connection with the land that Indigenous cultures do.

You know, I've been thinking about it, what you said the other day about even your own passing. As you said, you can't go back to that Buddhist temple, so who do you rely on? But then it's a vacuum! And everybody is confronted by that. So that's why the spiritual part of what I'm talking about is essential, that people try to find a way that doesn't replicate what they left, but that gives them another dimension. It's necessary that we have a spiritual connection.

I totally agree with you. That's also missing in the political world. People thinking as if they live forever, they don't really communicate with death.

And that's why, too, we're talking about this. For me, on a personal level, the ideal is to combine art, political struggle, and spirituality as one force. That's what I'm working toward, so to speak.

And the amount of change, I mean the amount of things that need to be tackled and changed is phenomenal. That's why I always say, revolution is not an event. It's a way of life. It's an all-encompassing understanding of what we need as a species, as human. The powers that be are preventing that, so we have to confront them at some point. However, like in that metaphor of the wall, we can't just smash into it. We have to dig under and collapse it. But to get people to understand that…

But I really feel that these conversations are helping me. Like I was afraid to use the word "spirituality" before. But I'm starting to realize what you mean by it. It's not just religion. It's like the existential ground that connects our living with the invisible whole. It's something we can hardly talk about.

And it's important to make it clear that it is religion that destroyed spirituality. It replaced it. Before religion, spirituality existed throughout the world. It was different, every people, every group, every tribe had a different understanding. There wasn't one pope, or one Dalai Lama, or one book. There were thousands of little understandings throughout the world. People were living spiritually. Without forcing others to follow their way.

I feel like our friends' endeavors trying to build community and other ways of living are crucial, but then that spiritual connectivity is missing.

And that missing bit may be the hardest to find. Other people took thousands of years to develop it. I don't think we have that much time.

No, but that's helpful to at least understand the problem. It's not just learning how to grow food or build a house.

That brings me to the point of the dilemma for me. I more or less went to join people that came before me. How difficult it must be, or how impossible it must be, for people to do it on their own. Without thousands of years. That's a real dilemma. Myself, I went somewhere else to learn. But if I couldn't do that…And I think about it a lot. I anguish over it. What can we, what can people do? I did something that I can't suggest everybody do. So it really is a big dilemma.

But the first step is to realize how important it could be. Then we'll have to worry about, how does it come about? But the first thing is to realize that there's something missing.

That's why the image of the quilt is helpful: you have to look for whatever you can find. It's not going to be a whole world, just these little pieces…

That you put together. You know, all I can say is that the dilemma is greater than anybody realizes. That's the only honest thing I can say. It's almost insurmountable.

But there's a story I could tell you. One time, when my wife and I were living in the wilderness, we were camped by an enormous rock, like at the bottom of a cliff. We had some psilocybin mushroom, so we took it. And we reached a point where it had an effect on us. And she said "why don't we climb that?" I said "yeah, why don't we?" So we started climbing. I mean we're talking, on the scale of one to ten for difficulty, this was a ten. It was *sheer*. So we were up, I don't know how far, maybe halfway. And we looked down: oh shit! We can't go back down. Then we looked up: uh-oh. We can't go up either! So we're right in the middle like, oh shit. It was a terrifying moment.

I said, "we have to go up. We can't go down. But don't look up! Just look this far ahead of you, to see where the next hold is. Don't even think about how far there is to go. Just look for the next grip." And we did that, for an hour or however long it took, we just kept going trying to find the next hand hold. Until finally we got to the top. That's what our struggle is.

That's quite a metaphor.

I never thought about it like that before, but that's what our struggle is. We just have to keep going. If you look to the top you'll say, "oh shit we're never gonna get there."

What did you do when you got to the top? Did you just collapse?

I don't think I've ever breathed that easily in my life. And then we realized there was a way down, in the back.

You found a better way to go down?

From the back it was sloped. The back was easy. The front was totally sheer.

With this metaphor it's making me wonder, if we ever make it, was there an easier way?

That part of the metaphor works only after you get to the top. But you have to get to the top. That is the struggle. So once we find a coalescence of all these different elements, like the people who are trying to learn from the Earth, and we get to what we consider to be the top…It's not really the top. But at least it's a place where we can breathe.

NOW

DAY TWENTY

Ben, one important thing we're learning is that your struggle is continuous. It's not just the '60s, like a symbolic past. Your practice continues in shifting environments, in resistance against this capitalist world. Like even if you're a lumberjack, you're still trying to create community which is very different from consumerist society.

Well, my emphasis from the beginning was the concept of totality. So I wouldn't define my concerns as just political. Or artistic, or spiritual. In other words, it was important to me that the whole picture be unified. That change, what we call revolution, wasn't about just the political. It's not sufficient to change things only politically. What does that mean, regime change? You have to change life! The way people think, what has meaning and doesn't have meaning… It's about life in its completeness.

I wanted to ask you too about the question of transmission. You've talked about people that have influenced you in different moments in your life. And now younger generations are reaching out to you, you're part of this long, intergenerational transmission of experience. Maybe you could talk

more about the kind of guidance that you found, like certain people that really helped you?

See the problem is that, I didn't learn or absorb from one person. Like there was somebody who really helped in the art world. And there were people who helped in the political world. And there were people who helped in the spiritual world. But they didn't know each other, like they had no sense of the connection. It all connected through me, in a sense, because it all entered me. So it got connected in me. But I don't know how to verbalize it…

Hearing your stories every week, I'm realizing your unique view of human relations also. Like your idea of family has a really organic relationship with other people, you can be sometimes a father, somebody's child, comrade, brother. This totality is understood also through relations you created, not just you as an individual. You created this space between people.

And it's really hard to define. I don't even know how to express it, in a way. I'm not sure what words to use. I feel like I'm not able to convey my sense of it in words.

You did it intuitively. You connected your desire to befriend different people, Black Panther people, Living Theater, Bookchin, kids in the street.

Well, it's even more extended than that. Like here, on this corner of the block, these guys downstairs that have the food stands, they're Egyptian. And the guys on the corner, the delicatessen, are Palestinian. And the guys around the corner are from Kashmir. And I have a personal relationship with them, like I don't see them as just…

When I went with you to the Kashmiri restaurant, it was like they knew you for decades.

Yeah, when I go in there, the guy that works there says "hey baba!" He calls me "baba." And it might seem superficial to some people, but to me, that is actually revolutionary. Like when I first went in there, you know how I look, cowboy hat, boots. I could tell they were like "what's he doing here," you know. But to me, the revolution, it's not only taking a gun (although that might be part of it) — but to go in there and have a personal relationship with people from Kashmir and show that not everybody in America is jingoistic. Or like when I go into the deli and see the Palestinians, or the Egyptian guys downstairs, they're all friendly with me, and I treat them all as important. As real entities, not just…

Not just food guys or something.

Yeah. And I don't know how to convey that in words. Like for instance, my wife used to do jewelry shows, and I used to go with her. And so obviously, when we'd go there, she and I were friendly with the people managing the show. But I was equally friendly with the guys working on the floor, like the stevedores and the guys cleaning. I was the only person there as a vendor that really had relations with them. And to me that was important. It wasn't like I was only talking to the management. The people who worked there knew me, and treated me like a friend, like "oh hi, you're back again!" You know, I can't explain it in words, how important that is to me. To move through life in a revolutionary way, means connected. It's not sufficient, but the simplest way to put it, like I always say: revolution is not an event. It's a way of life.

It's not just a single event.

It's your total existence! It's how you talk to people, and who you talk to, and how you move around in the world. For example I prefer going to the Kashmiri place, to me that is more revolutionary than going to a regular restaurant that's just about business. Like the fact that they have a section in the back where people can pray, they have little rugs, so that Muslims can go and pray five times a day. And so anybody could walk in! You don't have to be a customer eating. That was part of what drew me to them.

It's hard to put it into words. I try to combine my beliefs, and how I live, in a connected way. It's not like I think "oh well the revolution isn't happening," so I'll just go do any old thing and support capitalistic businesses. To me it's important to support people that are more human, and less commercial, in a sense. I don't know if that's an important point, but to me it was important. But you know, I'm reluctant to even mention it because other people might think "so what, who cares?"

Because you're talking about the living complexity. It's not like ideology or theory that works with abstracted categories. It's about how you relate to people as people, not as workers or as Marxists or whatever. But so my question then, for people like us, for the Kashmiris, for these actual people: what can we do? How can we help each other?

How to reproduce that is…it's almost a contradiction. You can't make it programmatic. So how do you encourage people to just live it? That's always been a real difficulty for me, how to convey this idea. You just live it. It's not like you proselytize it, or organize it.

Make a formula or methodology.

And so I always feel like a voice in the wilderness. I can't pass it on, like a doctrine. It's not doctrinaire. I can't say to somebody "okay well you have to…" I can transmit it by living it. But I can't tell somebody "this is what you should do."

The idea of totality is a little similar maybe. Totality is very hard to talk about. You have to just deal with it.

Yeah, it's hard to conceptualize.

It's invisible.

And that's the beauty of it, and that's the difficulty of it. For instance, the understanding that, on the cosmic level, we're not even a grain of sand. How do you tell people, "recognize that you're just a grain of sand?" They wanna be special! Human! But the cosmos doesn't care if you live or die, really. It's not even aware of you. The cosmic is not aware. Like say there's a tsunami, and a million people die. There's no conscious realization by the cosmos, like "well we're gonna have it, even if a million people die." It's just there! But how do you convey that? That this whole thing just lives! It just moves. You just move with it. Or get out of the way.

That's why I'm against written religious texts that are like, as if God came and told them. Well first of all, God doesn't talk. And second of all —

God doesn't care!

Or exist! There is no God walking around talking to anybody! And so that's the dilemma: how do you get across to people that there is no dogma? Only life.

It's interesting to hear you talk about the limitations of ideology. It makes a lot of sense to me from my experience in political milieus, like how disconnected people can become through their ideological interpretations. But when you talk about the spiritual world that you're part of, there doesn't seem to be the same problem, I guess?

Well the people I'm involved with, on the spiritual level, they have no dogma. It's experiential. It's a connection to…It's a connection to things, without a definition. And I think part of what happens, when people use words, like say on the political level, people talk about political concepts. But oftentimes the same word means something different to another person. And then words lock you in, they eliminate the fluidity. So it's easier to become antagonistic, to become enemies through words. But if you're dealing with people on some other level, there's a fluidity that is possible. I'm not saying that would work all the time. But there's a fluidity that's eliminated by words. That's why I'm opposed to religious texts. Because words don't breathe, they don't feel, they don't live. The word becomes a prison. Like people say the word will set you free — to me it's the opposite. The word will imprison you.

To be honest with you, I don't know if there's a solution. I don't know if people can evolve to a non-verbal…

But it's important that we talked about it, that there's this non-verbal dimension. We're living that dimension. Indescribable interrelations.

And the problem is that we use words to communicate, more than feeling. We can't eliminate verbal communication. But we could supplement it. Like say right now words are ninety percent of our communication — we could knock it down to fifty percent.

And more looking at each other, or facial expression, or body language.

Or vibe. As they said in the '60s, like "hey man, what's your vibe?" It's the feeling, it's the impression, the energy. So instead of talking to each other, they could feel each other's vibe.

What I struggle with in terms of the political atmosphere today, and I think a big problem for my generation in general, is this hyper-fixation on the self. And people have to sell themselves, everybody is desperate to have their little niche, like "this is me, this is my position." It's all about the self. So for me it's really meaningful to be able to talk with you and see a bigger picture.

Yeah. And I can't think of how to lay it out, other than what we're doing, meeting and talking like this. You know, there's no agenda, there's no organization.

Also you refuse to make a rule, you refuse to talk about a platform. Don't just talk about it, do it, right?

Live it, yeah. And it's like we talked about the other day, everybody has to find their way. That's the problem with dogma and ideology, they're based on a script that says "here, this is the way." But the path, it is you who must find it. In other words, what motivates me, I can't assume will motivate somebody else. If I tell you, maybe it's not right for you. So I can only tell you that you have to find it. I can't tell you what it is. I have to just be satisfied with spreading the idea that we all have to find it.

So it's a matter of setting markers — not defining the path, but setting out markers. A marker is ephemeral, it's not permanent. It's not like you're putting up a sign, THIS IS THE WAY. You're just putting a marker. People could ignore it, step over it, move it, I mean it's not like a sign post.

One thing that's wonderful about having this time together, hearing all these stories and reflections from your life, it becomes an example, like an illustration. It gives a glimpse of the fullness of experience. That helps at least to imagine what it is, to find a way. One's way.

It's never complete. I wish I had more time...There's so much. But, you know, we can't know these things when we're young, and have a lot of time. We learn these things as we go. So we end up toward the end saying "oh I wish I had more time to talk about what I learned." But it doesn't work that way.

You wish you had more time to transmit.

Yeah, to share it. And then, you can't even find anybody to listen to it!

But it seems that you're doing a lot, you're so active in the different worlds you're part of.

Yeah, but...I mean, I'd like to do even more. But I'm doing as much as I can. And I'm happy for it. But there's so much to do. Everything's so wrong. It's all wrong. They've gotten everything backwards. You know how long it's going to take to reverse it?

Sometimes I think this is the beginning of a long process of declining, toward the end.

But it is what it is. If while we're speaking there's some asteroid hurtling toward us, and it's going to crash into Earth, we don't even know it, and this conversation may actually be irrelevant. Because when it hits, we're gone!

And it's happened. Many, many times. Nothing is forever.

1000 voices is a publishing platform and tool for encounter, working to transmit and translate conversations about people's lives in struggle across the planet. More at 1000voices.info.

Anonymous by choice, **Ben Morea** was the force behind the legendary '60s groups Black Mask and Up Against the Wall Motherfucker. Since then his activities have inspired myriad retrospectives, interviews and publications. *Full Circle* is the most extensive account of his life and the only one authored by Morea himself.